So You Think You've Messed Up

God has a plan and a purpose for you!

Helen Rylance

Copyright @2021 by Helen Rylance

All rights reserved. No part of this book may be reproduced in any form or by any electronic or mechanical means, including information storage and retrieval systems, without permission in writing from the publisher, except by reviewers, who may quote brief passages in a review.

This publication contains the opinions and ideas of its author. It is intended to provide helpful and informative material on the subjects addressed in the publication. The author and publisher specifically disclaim all responsibility for any liability, loss or risk, personal or otherwise, which is incurred as a consequence, directly or indirectly, of the use and application of any of the contents of this book.

WORKBOOK PRESS LLC
187 E Warm Springs Rd,
Suite B285, Las Vegas, NV 89119, USA

Website:	https://workbookpress.com/
Hotline:	1-888-818-4856
Email:	admin@workbookpress.com

Ordering Information:
Quantity sales. Special discounts are available on quantity purchases by corporations, associations, and others.
For details, contact the publisher at the address above.

ISBN-13:   978-1-954753-59-4 (Paperback Version)
           978-1-954753-60-0 (Digital Version)

REV. DATE: 16/03/2021

CONTENTS

CHAPTER 1 1
CHAPTER 2 7
CHAPTER 3 17
CHAPTER 4 19
CHAPTER 5 22
CHAPTER 6 25
CHAPTER 7 34
CHAPTER 8 44
CHAPTER 9 48
CHAPTER 10 53
CHAPTER 11 59
CHAPTER 12 67
CHAPTER 13 70
CHAPTER 14 78
CHAPTER 15 82
CHAPTER 16 90
CHAPTER 17 97
CHAPTER 18 102
CHAPTER 19 105
CHAPTER 20 108
CHAPTER 21 113
CHAPTER 22 118
CHAPTER 23 123
CHAPTER 24 126

This book is dedicated to Robin and Vy who the Lord brought along side me for such a time as this. I am truly grateful to the Lord and to you both for being there for me. May He continue to use and bless you both.

We hope this book is a blessing to you. Those of us who have laboured together to produce it want to thank you for taking the time to read this story. So take a bow Sylvia, Ian, Ruth, Pam and Brenda. Not forgetting Maurice Barratt of Barratt Ministries. Without your help I would not have been able to produce this book. So a big thank you to you all. I am blessed to have had your support.

-Helen

Our lives can be compared to a river as it meanders on, sometimes through the peace and tranquility of the wide shallow places, at other times hurtling and crashing along as it meets boulders in the river bed. It can twist and turn so often that we lose sight of its destination as we are tossed about in its torrent. Still the Lord says *I know the plans and purpose I have for you.* Trust me.

This is the story of how Almighty God made promises to me at one of the lowest points of my life. Following a life filled with so many difficulties, culminating in divorce, I felt I had no future, I was without hope.

This book was written for all those who feel God could not possibly use them, to encourage you to believe that the Lord does have a plan and purpose that only you can fulfil. You have been uniquely equipped to fulfil His plan. Impossible! you say, then read on. For the Lord says, *I know the plans and purposes I have for you. Plans to prosper you not to harm you, plans to give you a hope and a future* (Jeremiah 29 v 11). When you read these words or see them as a text on calendars, fridge magnets or book marks have you ever wondered about the truth of these words? Do you really believe them? When your life has fallen apart and all your dreams are in ashes at your feet, can you still believe what the Lord says through the prophet Jeremiah?

There are times in our life when tragedy strikes and we lose our home, our family, someone we love dearly, our self esteem, our place in the church, the respect of others, our job. There are so many apparent tragedies just waiting to happen. How then can we be sure that God will be faithful to His promises?

How did Joseph feel when he was thrown into a pit, rejected by his brothers, wrongly accused by Potiphar's wife, and then ended up in prison? Did he continue to believe the revelations that God had given him so many years before?

When Abraham and Sarah still didn't have the child they had been promised ten years after the promise was given, did they hang on to the promises of God? When God promised to make Abraham the father of nations, and of a people more numerous than the stars, how did he feel all those years later, still waiting for God to fulfil his promise?

If you find it hard to accept those whose lives have not been run on the lines that you expect Christian lives to be run on, then this book is for you! The lives of many of Jesus' descendants were frequently less than perfect. You and I are no different to these Biblical characters. Their lives are recorded to encourage us and to make us realise that we too can overcome by the grace of God and come into all that He has planned for us.

CHAPTER 1

Mine was a home birth; we lived in a house that had all mod cons even in 1940. Our home was in a Lancashire seaside town. Immediately after my birth my mother experienced a severe mental breakdown and had to be taken to hospital in a straight jacket. This was my welcome to the world. At my birth the placenta clung to my face and I nearly died. The midwife later declared it was thought to be lucky to be born in this way. To this day I can't understand how it can be lucky to nearly die at birth!

After that auspicious start, Mum was taken to the mental ward of the hospital and I went to the baby unit.

Mum was pregnant with me when my parents got married. There had been a lot of ill feeling over my conception. To be pregnant before marriage in the 1940's was considered to be a tremendous disgrace. My Mum was the youngest of two sisters; her sister was married and gave birth to her daughter at the beginning of the same month that I was born. My conception spoilt everything for my aunt, uncle and grandparents and they never let me forget that. Many years later the Lord showed me why they didn't like me and asked me to forgive them, which by His grace I was able to do.

The second world war was in full swing when I was born, Mum and I were in hospital for six weeks in all, only coming together when an air raid was taking place. Mum was very fearful of the Germans and their bombs and consequently I became a child full of fears who lacked bonding with her Mother and who was rejected by her Mother's family. The women of the family, Grandmother, Mum and my aunt were hardworking but hard, cruel women. My cousin and I are the same age, she was an only child whilst I was the eldest of eight children. When my cousin's mother died I was surprised when she told me how controlling and cruel her mother had been. Whilst I had experienced that side of her nature toward myself, I was surprised her only child had received the same treatment.

My parents were also hardworking people, particularly my dad who would do anything for my mother. To the extent it would lead him into a life of crime in order to supply her with the lifestyle she craved. A big house, cars, furs, antique furniture to name but a few things he provided from his criminal life style. When he was caught and imprisoned on two occasions, their marriage broke down and they divorced. He never committed a crime again. In later life he admitted he had been weak to give in to my mum's desires.

CHANGES

When I was eleven years old we moved from our lovely big home in the country to a mill town in Lancashire and reduced to living in a back to back terraced house with an outside loo and no bathroom. What a comedown from the beautiful four bedroom detached home in its own grounds with a smallholding for pigs and poultry. The shock from the change of environment was immense. However, nothing to compare with the bullying I received from the pupils at the school I attended who knew of my father's imprisonment. That had all now been left behind along with my childhood.

On my tenth birthday my mother had declared ' I was a big girl now, no more playing, I had to help clean the house and look after the then four other children with the fifth due any day.

Illness had plagued me all my young days; chickenpox, measles etc., and they always had some other problem attached to them, pnuemonia, mastoids etc would complicate these childhood illnesses, making them life threatening.

When I was nine years old we were having a family day out when I stood on a piece of glass hidden in the sand; I shrieked and jumped onto my dad's back. He didn't realise I was hurt and thought I was being silly. Looking around he realised how bad the situation was. My parents wrapped a towel around my foot as dad and I set off to find a doctor. No mean feat on a sunny Sunday afternoon in the summer, in an isolated coastal area and finally after driving around for more than an hour, he managed to find a doctor who put sixteen stitches in the wound. The tendon was severed but eventually, after several months of hobbling around, I learned to walk again, though it was many years before I could put full pressure on my injured foot.

Six months later I developed Rheumatic fever. I was paralysed for three months, unable to move any part of my body. I believe this was a result of a combination of circumstances I was unable to cope with.

Both my parents had been educated in the Grammar School system and they wanted the same type of education for me, but I wasn't able to cope with the pressure of their expectations and fulfil their hopes. Furthermore, my schooling had been greatly disrupted by illness and I had become increasingly nervous by the bullying I was being subjected to. As a result, on the day my dad dropped me off at the school where the exam was taking place, I was in no fit state to take the exam. When the exam was over dad took me to see the film 'Red Shoes', which I loved. That night was the last time I would walk or move for more than three months. My life became one of fear and pain, loneliness and isolation. This was to become the pattern of my life for many years to come, through this illness, which would attack my body every time I felt under pressure and unable to cope.

RESPONSIBILITY

As my Mother became a lone parent with six children, my life became one of all work and little play. There was little time for playing between cleaning the house, washing and ironing as well as carrying out a part time job to help feed the family, and of course my schooling. However I did have one friend—Pam. She lived at the pub next door. One year when we were about twelve we had matching dresses, for me this was a great thrill as new clothes were a rarity. Another time we set up a pulley system between her house and ours, we used to send packets of chips from the shop mum had. The Fish and Chip shop mum had bought, was failing and soon closed. Mum started going out and met several men and soon child number seven was on the way. We six children lived in squalor in the bedrooms. Mum slept downstairs with her lover, who eventually became husband number two. Finally, we moved to better quality housing through having been allocated a council house which had a good sized garden. By this time I was fourteen years of age and I was able to give up my part time work. Now I had more time to make friends and enjoy a teenager's life with friends and boyfriends.

When I left school I had wanted to go on to higher education. I had been offered a place to study Domestic Science. However, mum said they couldn't afford for me to go to college so I would have to think of some other type of work. I really didn't know what else I wanted to do. One day I was shopping in town and decided to pop into Boots Chemist, and see if they had any vacancies, and after an interview, I was offered a job as a sales assistant. A few weeks later I was promoted to an apprentice to study dispensing medicine.

The following year my mother was pregnant again, this time she was taken to hospital as she suffered a miscarriage. It was during this time that my stepfather decided I needed some sex education. For several years, when he had been out drinking at night, he would come to my bedroom. He would try and put his hands under the bedclothes to touch me. I got wise to this and used to wrap the bedclothes tightly round my shoulders to prevent this. I would pretend to be asleep and not answer him when he called my name. Finally, with mum in hospital he made his move. Waking me in the middle of the night he called me into his bedroom, where he was sat on the bed, naked. I was terrified and became hysterical, which no doubt saved me from further abuse. He wanted me to touch him. I was thoroughly shocked and shaken by this incident and cried frequently. Over the following weeks I would regularly break down crying. My stepfather had threatened he would tell my Mum it was my fault, that it was I who came onto him, so I kept quiet and said nothing.

Eventually, I could keep it to my self no longer and told my mum what had happened She didn't believe me and she did blame me just as my stepfather had said. When her marriage broke down after her eighth child was born she said it was my fault because of this incident with my stepfather.

Soon I was engaged to my first husband. While I loved him I know that had we waited to marry until after my twenty first birthday as we had intended, I would not have married him. Whilst he was a good man, he did have temper tantrums especially with his mother. He frequently threw items or cleared the table of it pots and things in a fit of temper. However, he didn't, at this time, demonstrate this side of his nature towards me.

We had become sexually active after our engagement, this was another reason I felt I could not break off our engagement as I felt no other man would want me.

That year was awful. Mum was not speaking to me, blaming me for her marriage breakdown. She would frequently not speak to me for a month at a time, then when I was in the 'good books', my step father was out of them and she wouldn't speak to him. Life was a constant 'tell her this', 'tell him that'. It was emotionally wearing. I was only allowed out three or four nights a week and had strict time deadlines for being home. I invariably wept for half the evening such was the tension I lived through at that time.

TEARS

On our wedding day I wept so much that the vicar had to stop the service, as I sought to control my sobs, but married we were.

Six months after our wedding my husband and I had a row, words were exchanged and blows struck by us both. I walked the streets in the pouring rain not knowing what to do. I knew if I went back I would have to be submissive and not answer back. Just as I thought I was free from my mother's control and domination I found myself with a husband who likewise did not like a wife with an opinion or voice, should I leave or submit was the dilemma. I went back having vowed to myself to keep the peace come what may. This I must have managed to do because it was another nineteen years before I received another beating. I didn't challenge anyone, I submitted to whatever was required of me and learned not to answer back. So we lived happily like that producing three lovely children, until his attention began to stray.

CHAPTER 2

My dad had gone out of our lives after my parents divorce, On the rare occasion he could afford to visit us we were made so fearful of him by our mother that we would hide behind the furniture and not come out until my dad had left. This must have been very hurtful for him. dad who was a lovely loving man, finally gave up trying to contact us. When I was sixteen he turned up at the shop I worked at, but sadly because of my fear, I was unable to meet him. However, when I was twenty one he wrote to me and we were reconciled. After that we had many happy years together. However, Mum wasn't happy about our meeting. She had found out about our meetings through going through my mail when visiting our home. He however, despite marrying again, loved her to the end and regretted their separation.

Our first son was born four years after our marriage. It was a long protracted birth leaving me ill and exhausted, with a child who cried a lot and slept little. When our second son was born, again it was a long labour but not as tiring. We decided to have him christened at the local Methodist Church which my neighbour attended. The Pastor of the Church challenged me about sending our eldest son to Sunday School whilst not attending myself. This was the start of my seeking for something more to life. Sadly I didn't see it in the people in this Church, because I was spiritually blind, even in my friend who prayed for me to come to know Jesus. However, when we moved to a different area of town and attended another Church, Jesus met with me.

JESUS BREAKS IN

It was a Thursday in late August and I was washing the breakfast pots after taking my eldest son to school; the baby was asleep in his pram. Two days previously I had attended the first of what was to be an ongoing ladie's Bible study. After the meeting Anne, the lady whose home the meeting was held in, approached me and asked if I was Christian. I said I was, but when she spoke of Jesus becoming my Saviour I realised I wasn't sure. For the following two nights I couldn't sleep , I was so challenged by the thought of Jesus coming into my life. Finally, on that Thursday morning I called out to Jesus and said if He was real would He please come into my life. The peace that came with Jesus was immense, I had never known anything like it. This was it, I was born again of the Spirit of God. I was a new creation!

Almost immediately I developed a deep depression, what I didn't know then was my great, great, grandmother had been a spiritualist medium. God says to dabble in these things is sin and brings a curse on a family. Eventually after three years this was lifted; as I learned to quote scripture at Satan, the depression left. During that three years I began to teach the scriptures to children and also helped with the ladie's meeting.

REVELATION

It was around this time I began to take the scripture at its word. When it spoke about being baptised by immersion, I looked into it and sought the Lord. A friend and I were baptised with a group of Christians from our home town. The denomination we worshipped in did not believe or encourage adult baptism, in fact when we were baptised we were ostracised by our fellow worshippers, particularly the leaders; this was very upsetting for us. However, within two years we saw each one of them come into baptism.

HEALING

Healing was something else I noticed Jesus did. At the time I had a heart condition which I had been told was something I would have all my life. However, when I sought the Lord regarding healing , he said just wait until I say the word and I will heal you, and he did just that. A few months later I had to have a minor operation to remove a cyst from my shoulder. On that day the Lord told me to stop taking my heart medication. This is not something readers should do without a word from the Lord. From that day onward I didn't need any medication, and in later years I was advised not to declare the heart problem to insurers as there was no evidence of any heart complaint.

Then I saw in the Bible something about being Baptised in the Holy Spirit. When I prayed about it the Lord led me to a local fellowship who, for the coming six weeks, were going to study this subject. I attended their mid-week fellowship and received the teaching offered. At the end the vicar laid hands on me and I received a powerful infilling of the Holy Spirit. I didn't speak in tongues at the time; this came a year or two later as I sought the Lord for more of this gift. However, from this powerful infilling I could praise the Lord for hours, it just bubbled up like a stream of living water a great joy and blessing.

ME

By this time I had made several good friends through work and amongst former neighbours, some of which I am still in contact with forty years later. My dad had a love of gardening and I have inherited this. Much of my spare time is spent gardening or visiting garden centres. The love of nature is such a blessing.

I love children, particularly my own and our fifteen grandchildren. Sadly much of what I have learned about good parenting came too late in life to influence my own children. Having said that, by

God's grace they have become three lovely caring adults. However, it does come in handy with our many grandchildren who I am able to encourage and affirm far more than I did their parents. My three children all know the Lord and have done so since they were children. Both my sons recommitted their lives to the Lord in their teens, serving the Lord by preaching and teaching, the youngest is a Pastor in the south of England.

FAITH

My daughter had a wonderful faith as a child. She would pray for healing and very much believed the Lord would hear her and He did. Once she had broken her arm, she asked if I thought the Lord would heal it for her. When I replied yes, she went off to her bedroom and when she returned, she said she had prayed. A week later we had to return to the hospital for a second x-ray. We noticed the doctor was puzzling over the x-ray. He said 'I don't understand this, her arm was definitely broken, but now it is healed.'

At that time we had an unreliable car which she frequently prayed over when it broke down, then we would see it spring back to life. Sadly when she was thirteen a curse that was on the family line kicked in , though at the time I was unaware of it. All I knew was I had a very rebellious teenager whose life was out of control. The rejection she experienced at birth from her father had much to do with the path she took. However, little by little the Lord is drawing her back to Himself.

It is out of this background this story has been written, as I went about my daily life. A life of plenty and poverty, of abuse and cruelty both physically and verbally from almost every authority figure in my life.

When Father God came into my life, I saw Him not as one who loved me unconditionally but as one like my mother, whose lack of love and care ran through most of my life. She had inherited this from her mother. The matriarchal spirit that controls her and through which she seeks to control people and situations has run long and hard down our family line. However, I am glad to say that I have never had any desire to control people, rather my desire is to affirm all people and see them set free to become the people Jesus intended them to be.

I have made many mistakes, mistakes as a daughter, wife, mother and friend. The joy of knowing my Saviour has forgiven me my past sins as I embrace the Cross of Christ and receiving His resurrection life has enabled me to move on with Him to accomplish His plans and purposes.

I WAS AMAZED

I remember the day clearly when the Lord told me I would write this book. It was my thirty sixth birthday and the Lord had just told me that later in my life I would write a Christian book. "Lord I said what could I possibly have to write about, mine is such an ordinary life?" That was about to change and seemingly for the worst. All the Lord said at the time was. "You will have something to write about but first you must live it."

It had all started when my daughter was six weeks old. It was early afternoon and I had felt this terrible tearing within me. The pain was so intense that I cried out to the Lord. In my heart there was this intense pain, but the words in my mind were even more painful. 'There is something terribly wrong with my marriage', was running through my mind. What could be wrong? We were an ordinary family. Yes, the past few months had been difficult.

TRIALS

In January one of my brothers had been killed in a freak accident, it was the first year we had experienced very powerful gales in the winter, much damage had been done throughout the land and several people had been killed. Charles was one of those. He had got up early to go to the fruit and vegetable market to buy in the produce for the wholesaler he worked for. It was a wild , windy morning and the wagon rocked as he drove to the city market. When he arrived, he parked up and tied the doors back on the wagon in readiness to load up the vehicle with the fruit and vegetables he had called for. He had just started loading the carrots onto the wagon when a mighty gust of wind snapped the rope holding the door back. Charles was bending over the wagons tail board when the door whipped back hitting him across his back and knocking him to the ground. Winded he got to his feet and went to get more carrots only to collapse on the ground. He didn't know his liver had been ruptured; he was rushed to the hospital but within half an hour he was dead. A man who was an exceptionally fit athlete, was gone in no time at all. He was a well known international cyclist, but even his fitness could not save him from that fatal blow.

I was three months pregnant at the time and was still in bed when my mum came early that morning to tell me of his death I just couldn't take it in, but it was true, my best mate was gone. Charles and I had always had a good rapport, we had even said if we had not been brother and sister we would like to have married each other. Not that there was ever anything wrong with our relationship, it was as it should be brother and sister, but we admired each other greatly. Two months later my dad, suffered a massive stroke which left him paralysed and unconscious for a month before his death. In the midst of all this I had realised that my husband was not being very supportive. He was not present at the birth of our daughter, and when he came to visit us after her arrival he made some derogatory remark about her face and left after a few minutes, saying he was going to tell a woman whom he had become friendly with at work, that she had been born. I was so shocked I didn't ask why he wasn't first going to tell our children or our parents. There were no flowers or congratulations from my husband, no close moments, or cuddles for the new addition to our family. Just that 'I must go and tell Dorothy'. Our daughter wailed constantly and needed a lot of comforting. Fortunately, as our sons were older and needed less attention as they were at school during the day, I was able to give her the comfort she needed. Looking back I realise that even as a baby she was aware of the rejection that had been spoken over her at birth, by her father.

AGONY

It was a Thursday when I became aware of the tearing pain in my heart, it was agonising, was I having a heart attack? No. Such was the anguish I felt I needed help, so I telephoned my Pastor who was a good pastoral man. Sensing my distress he came round to our home immediately and prayed with me. He could offer no explanation for what I had experienced at that time. I had been married fourteen years.

Some months later I met another Christian lady who told me she had experienced the same thing, her husband had been having an affair and had committed adultery, this was when she too had experienced this same pain. I knew that my husband had become very close to a lady he worked with, but I had pushed it out of my mind and I had no reason to assume that his relationship with this woman was anything but friendship. Jesus said that when two people marry they become one flesh. Does this mean that when one partner commits adultery the two are torn apart? It would seem so, He went on to say; that which we join ourselves to, we become one with. Therefore it seems logical that there is inevitably a tearing apart. But had he committed adultery? I had no way of knowing. He occasionally went to this lady's house and even took the boys on occasions. He spoke of her often, discussed things with her and increasingly excluded me. It was to be another twenty years before a pastor told me that my experience was that of a close tie being formed with another person outside of the marriage, as when one person falls in love with another or commits adultery either way he said the bond between us had been broken at that time.

After struggling for a further seven years to keep my first marriage alive, to a man who eventually said that he did not want me, and had no desire to make our marriage work, I was on my own with three children. Like many women before me and since, I found a job and got on with my life. Soon the financial burden of buying a house on one wage became too much. I had bought my ex-husbands half of the house leaving myself with a large mortgage. I prayed and sought advice from church leaders. Our fellowship had become involved with a project building flats for elderly people. I was part of the project team, I was asked by our Pastor if I would like the job of warden, caring for the elderly. There was a flat for the warden big enough for me and the children. So we rented our house out and moved into the flat. The children and I enjoyed ministering to the elderly people who lived there, seeing several in their eighties come to know the Lord and be baptised as believers. However, being on duty twenty four hours a day, with three children to look after became too much. Eventually I resigned and we moved into a council flat, it was here that the Lord gave me a vision for the future.

Could I, would I believe the Lord, if I did how would I come into what he had promised? Why does the Lord give us these revelations? If we look at the lives of Abraham and Sarah, Joseph, Jonah and others, we will recognise that these people also received words of comfort during dark and difficult days. Revelations and visions can encourage us when life is difficult seemingly without hope. Jeremiah chapter 29v11 tell us that the Lord's plans are to give us a hope and a future. That hope and future are found through verses 12 and 13.

What a loving heavenly Father we have who knows us so well that He gives us encouragement in the darkest times of our lives, when he tells us he has a plan and purpose for us, and I have discovered that he means it.

ORDINARY WOMEN

I am just an ordinary woman, who has worshipped the Lord and walked with Him for more than thirty five years.

There are ordinary women whose lives are recorded in the Bible. Joanna, wife of Cuza the manager of Herod's household, Susanna and many others. Mary Magdalene was also part of this group of ladies who were to meet Jesus practical every day needs providing food for Him, maybe even doing His washing. Mary came from a tiny village situated on the edge of the sea of Galilee. We are told of this in Luke chapter eight vs 1-3 *The twelve were with him and also some women who had been cured of evil spirits and diseases, Mary called Magdalene from whom seven demons had been cast out, Joanna the wife of Cuza, the manager of Herod's household, Susanna, and many others.* These women were helping to support them out of their own means. Mary's former life style as a prostitute resulted in her becoming demon possessed. Jesus set her free. Her love for the Lord came from a grateful heart, when the Lord sets the captive free they invariably have a grateful heart, a heart full of love for Him. We are told he who is forgiven much, loves much. A heart that has love seeks to pour that love out on the Saviour just as Mary did when she poured the costly ointment on Jesus feet, using her hair to wipe his feet, using what she had to bless the Lord with.

God had a plan and purpose for these women and they came into that which he had planned for them.

When we study the genealogy of Jesus we find his ancestors were far from perfect. Look at David later to become King David he committed adultery and had a man murdered. What about Rahab? She was a prostitute and a liar and the Lord used her in his plans. He used her to protect the two spies who were there to spy out the land. Then there is Tamar who tricked and seduced her father in law, then bore illegitimate twins. Many others on Jesus family line had what we would consider to be shady pasts.

Maybe you are in the latter years of your life and are wondering what your life has been about. Simeon and Anna were in their eighties when they fulfilled God's plan and purpose for them.

The Lord has promised that when our hair is grey our lives will be fruitful.

CHAPTER 3

It was on a cold February day in 1984 that I received the revelation or vision that was to change my life. I was relaxing in a chair, just resting before the Lord. I saw a house, it was the style of house I like, a modern Georgian detached house in its own grounds. In the Spirit I went into the house and saw that it had five bedrooms, one was on the ground floor the remainder were on the upper floor. There were bathrooms and separate washrooms with toilets. One bathroom always remained in my mind. It had a dark green bath, toilet and washbasin and the walls and ceiling were lined with pine wood— it was a lovely room. The remaining rooms included a lounge, kitchen and laundry. While I didn't see the back garden I had the impression that it was a very special place. There was a driveway on the left of the house with a car on the drive. I knew in the vision that I was married, though at the time I received the vision I was divorced.

The word the Lord gave me was *and strangers will come to your door.* With it came a strong impression that the house was for ministry.

With great joy I received this vision, and praised the Lord as I excitedly thought of what had been revealed to me, expecting it to come into being very soon.

Looking back I have appreciated the encouragement of this vision, which kept me moving on walking with the Lord despite some of the darkest and most difficult years of my life some of which I am going to share with you in the coming chapters. Yet like Abraham and Sarah, I had taken wrong turnings as I sought to come into the vision. Some may say mistakes were made as I attempted to find the house that I had seen in the vision. There was a lot to learn, not just about visions, but most of all about the Lord and myself. He was to say many times over the years to come. *My ways are not your ways, My thoughts are not your thoughts.*

Hindsight is a wonderful gift given to us after an event. Abraham and Sarah may well have thought so too when they looked back on their lives and the mistakes they made , some quite blatant, like lying, others out of frustration at the delays in God's plans, delays they did not understand. It does not matter how many seeming mistakes we make along the way the Lord takes them and weaves them into that perfect tapestry He has designed. A tapestry that ultimately will show that He has, and is ever conforming us to the image of His son, the Lord Jesus Christ.

The gloom of that time receded for a while as I basked in the glow of thoughts of the future, to have a nice house again to be with someone who loved me, and to have a work from the Lord was encouraging, there was hope, light at the end of the dark tunnel that I was in. Never having had a vision or revelation before I didn't know what to do next. So I shared it with a friend.

CHAPTER 4

Many people fail to come into the visions or revelations given by the Lord because of their failure to commit themselves to the process the Lord has laid down for us in scripture. Samson is a classic example. Though he was ordained from the womb to be a man greatly used of God, we may consider that he failed miserably, though this would be far from the truth because scripture tells us differently. His parents brought him up as they had been instructed by an angel. However, Samson had a weakness for women, this lead him from the path ordained for him. Despite this in his final hours on earth he fulfilled his purpose by killing more of Israel's enemies in his death than in his entire life.

LOSING OUR VISION

In Habakkuk chapter 2 v 3 it says *Without vision the people perish* Samson lost his vision and so perished. Samson also lost his mobility as he was bound with fetters.

We too can become bound by sin, or even people. When sin comes in repentance is the only answer. When we turn away from sin and repent, if we get right with the Lord, He will forgive and restore us.

People can cause us to lose our vision or even rob us of our vision. We need to be careful whom we share our precious things with. People can sometimes get hold of the wrong end of the stick and cause problems for us. The jealousy of others can cause you to abandon that which the Lord has given you.

Adam lost respect for himself when he sinned. He became independent of God and did what he wanted. I can't say that I ever deliberately went my own way during the period of waiting for the vision to come into being, but I obviously did make mistakes, because my thoughts were on occasions not Gods thoughts.

When you begin to lose sight of your vision call out to the Lord to restore the vision to you and he will. *Remember though the vision tarry, wait for it* (Habakkuk chapter 2 v 3).

Sharing a vision in the early stages is not the wisest thing to do, as I was soon to discover.

The response of our closest friends on these occasions can be dampening to say the least

SHARING THE VISION

However, we learn by experience, so we are told. I learned fast not to share these things. Having shared the vision with two Christian friends, on separate occasions, what did they do? They laughed, "Why would the Lord give you a big house?" They asked. At that time my self esteem was very low, so I agreed with them. Why would the Lord give me a big house and a husband as well as a ministry? This only happened to special people and I wasn't one of those, were my thoughts. I was a nobody, with little or no future! They were right. So I laid the vision down believing it to be impossible, but I reckoned without God.

Two months later at a church meeting, a visiting Pastor gave me a word of knowledge about seeking the Lord regarding my future. Encouraged I set time aside to seek the Lord and much to my surprise he gave me back the vision he had shown me previously. This time I thanked Him and took hold of it with both hands. I wasn't going to let go of it again, no matter how many people laughed and ridiculed me.

JOB

Job had friends who thought they were helping him by their remarks. Initially they were supportive, they sat by him for seven days, they wept with him, and sat silently with him, no doubt pondering what he had done to deserve this trouble. God had called Job blameless and upright. yet in (Job chapter 8 v 20) one of the friends says *surely God does not reject a blameless man or strengthen the hands of evil doers,* By the end of the story the Lord rebukes the friends, and tells Job to pray for them. We too must forgive those who don't see as we see, hear as we hear.

What should you do with a vision or revelation? I didn't know, so I started to make enquiries of those I thought would have the answer.

One Pastor told me that if it didn't happen within a short period of time, it meant it wasn't of the Lord. Another pastor told me of a vision he had, which was of a particular church building and he believed it was an indication from the Lord that he was going to Pastor that particular fellowship. He had been seeking the Lord regarding moving to another fellowship, so he began to apply for vacant posts. Eventually he was called to preach at the fellowship he had seen in the vision, but he wasn't appointed as Pastor to that fellowship. He was very discouraged by this and as a result he eventually left the ministry.

SEEKING THE LORD

It is obviously necessary to seek the Lord until we are fully assured of His desire for us. I knew then that I was to give myself to prayer and seek the Lord until the vision was manifest. How long does it take to bring a vision or revelation to birth?

CHAPTER 5

Praying a vision into being is a bit like being pregnant. You wonder when it will end. Day by day it continues along its allotted course. Are the doors of heaven made of brass? It seems like it on occasions, does the Lord hear? Of course He does, but visions and revelations are not birthed in a day.

The intensity and frequency of prayer were such, that I used to call it the magnificent obsession because I couldn't get away from it. When I went to bed it was there, if I woke in the night it was still there. I would even wake up praying. Finally, when I woke in the morning it was still there. Just as we grow bigger in pregnancy so too this grew. One year after another went by and finally after almost three years it was nearly time to bring it to birth.

HELP COMES

At that time the Lord brought into my life Rev Gary Stevenson. Gary was a missionary and itinerant preacher. He would preach the word of the Lord in our fellowship two or three times a year. Each time the Lord would encourage me through him I used to feel these sermons were just for me, I was so blessed. The Lord spoke into my life several times through his sermons. This Sunday was no exception, he announced he was going to speak on handling revelations and visions. Wow! Thank you Lord, this is just what I need, and so it proved to be a word in season, just where I was at.

After the service I was able to talk to Gary about my vision, telling him how I just could not stop praying into it, despite the fact that almost three years had gone by since the Lord had given it to me. He encouraged me to keep praying, as he believed I was nearly at break through point— he was right Ten days later the praying came to an end and the birthing was over. I heard the Lord saying, "It is ratified in heaven, now bring it down to earth." "How do I do that", I asked, then it came to me to start praising the Lord and thank Him for bringing me this far. So I started to praise the Lord for all he had done, for all that the vision contained, expecting any day to receive the house and all I had seen.

CART BEFORE THE HORSE

One evening while praying with friends about the vision, the Lord showed my friends a picture of a horse and cart, showing the cart before the horse! The Lord was showing us that the house was not the prime thing we should pray for, but a husband.

However, as many readers will know, when the Lord reveals something of His plans and purposes for our lives. He also has to do a lot of preparation in the circumstances of our lives and many changes to our character are needed.

Joseph and Moses are but two who had long years of preparation to go through, before they were equipped to handle the responsibility that was to be theirs. Did they realise as they languished in prison or on the back of the desert that the Lord was preparing them for the future plans He had prepared for them? No of course not. For many years I did not recognise what was happening in my life. For fourteen years if I asked the Lord where my life was leading, He would say "Abraham knew not where he was going but he went."

Moses went through forty years of training before he could be trusted with leading the children of Israel out of Egypt.

Joseph spent many years in prison before he was changed from a youth, who was so conceited and bragged so much his brothers hated him, to a wise and humble man made ready to implement the rationing system to save Egypt and ultimately his own family from starvation.

So it is with us, it is foolish to think that we can come into positions of responsibility without being made ready by the Lord. The Lord has to take us through the hard school of knocks before conforming us to His Son's image as part of the changes that need to be made.

CHAPTER 6

The Bible tells us of several different ways the Lord reveals Himself and His plans and purposes for us, to us. Guidance can come in the form of visions, revelations, similitude, dreams, through the body of Christ or through reading the word of God, The Holy Bible.

What a wonderful Heavenly Father we have who has given us a variety of means of communicating His will to us. When we need encouragement, guidance or a fresh revelation of His love or glory, He is able to meet our needs. Sometime our frailty or weakness keeps us from seeing what the Lord is trying to reveal to us. Dreams can be given to lead us or guide us.

DREAMS

Joseph seems to be a name synonymous with dreams. Jacob's son was known as The Dreamer, maybe his dreams were given to sustain him during the times of hatred he experienced from his brothers. In the Bible in the book of Genesis it tells us that Joseph's brothers not only hated him, it says they couldn't speak a good word about him and this was before he had his famous dream. My mother was one of the people who couldn't speak well of me. During my waiting period I frequently preached in local churches. It was the custom in those days to put a short report in the local newspaper stating who had spoken and the subject matter. At that time my mother was working in the village newsagents, and could be frequently heard saying 'I see she's got her name in the paper again' in a derogatory fashion. It was very hurtful to have my mother speak in this manner, particularly as she had become a Christian.

JOSEPH

Another person whose dreams are recorded in the Bible is Joseph who was betrothed to Mary the mother of Jesus, and when she was found to be pregnant, scripture tells us in the book of Matthew *that because Joseph her husband was a righteous man and did not want to expose her to public disgrace,* he had decided in his own mind to divorce her quietly. Then an angel appeared to him in a dream and told him to *forget this idea, because the child Mary was carrying was conceived by the Holy Spirit. Later when Jesus was a baby and King Herod had decided to have all the baby boys under two years of age killed, hoping to catch Jesus in this mass murder ensuring that Jesus did not fulfil God's plan for Him. Joseph again had a dream. An angel told him to take Mary and the baby to Egypt.*

GIDEON

Dreams are frequently used to guide us. Gideon overheard a dream that had been given to encourage this timid warrior. When God first spoke to Gideon through an angel, Gideon was threshing wheat in the winepress. Why was he hiding in the winepress secretly threshing wheat? Because he was afraid the Midianite army would find the wheat that had obviously been overlooked by them. The book of Judges chapter 6 v 2-6 tells us The Midianite army was so oppressive, they ruined crops and slaughtered the animals, everyone lived in fear of them including Gideon.

AN ANGEL

The angel told Gideon that he was going to be used by God to defeat the Midianite army. Needless to say Gideon responds by stating how weak and unsuited he was to the call. (Judges Chapter 6 v 15). Finally, after convincing Gideon that the Lord is with him, and leaving him with an army of just 300 men, the Lord encourages him by telling Gideon to go down to the enemy camp and listens to what they are saying. It is recorded in Judges chapter 7 v 13-15. Just as Gideon arrived at the enemy camp a man was telling a friend his dream I had a dream. He was saying. A round loaf of barley bread came tumbling into the Midianite camp. It struck the tent with such force that the tent overturned and collapsed. His friend responded, This can be nothing other than the sword of Gideon son of Joash, the Israelite. God has given the Midianites and the whole camp into his hands. When Gideon heard the dream and it's interpretation, he worshiped God. He returned to his own men, telling them to get up as the Lord was going to give the Midianites and the whole camp into their hands. We can see that while we are sleeping God can speak to us, building us up and guiding us.

We still need to seek the Lord for an interpretation of our dreams as Daniel did and as Gideon experienced where the interpretation was explained.

ANOTHER DREAM

I have had several dreams when the Lord has been speaking to me regarding a course of action I was about to take. On one occasion my husband and I had been praying with another couple for about three months about a work we wanted to develop together. The Lord during that time had spoken to me regarding certain problem areas in what we were planning to do, but I was inclined to think that I was imagining things and ignored the warnings. Finally, in a dream, the Lord graciously showed me a picture of myself giving birth to a baby, with no feet. When I sought the Lord as to what the interpretation of the dream was, He told me the work we were praying about was not of Him and we were not to get involved. Immediately after having the dream, we had to go overseas for two weeks, we said nothing to our friends about the dream, preferring to pray privately about the situation while we were away. What a shock we had on our return to find our friends had gone ahead and started the work without us, despite the fact we had agreed previously not to implement anything without total agreement between us. During our stay overseas the Lord had shown us that there was a lack of integrity about our friends that we had been unwilling to accept previously because of our love for them, even though we had been aware of it. Within weeks the work our friends had started, collapsed leaving them devastated. The Lord in His graciousness will speak, if only we will let Him and be willing to listen. We are grateful to the Lord for stopping us from entering into something that would have distracted us from His plan and purpose for us. Listen to your dreams check them out it might be the Lord speaking.

THROUGH HIS WORD

The Lord frequently speaks to us through His word. We may be reading the scriptures when suddenly we are aware of the words leaping out of the page at us. We know the Lord is speaking to us through His word, when this happens we should make a record of it. Seeking the Lord as to its meaning. Though often when this happens it is a direct answer to prayers made previously. Another way that the Lord speaks through His word is by repeating the same verses twice. Some of the promises Abraham received were given to him twice, in the book of Genesis chapter 17 v 19 and chapter 18 v 10, it tells of the child promised to Abraham and Sarah. Elsewhere in Genesis the Lord says I confirm my word by repeating it. Psalm 118 has many repetitive patterns, this is the Lord's way of reinforcing what He has to say is important and we should pay attention when we come across such patterns.

FACE TO FACE

Few people meet with the Lord face to face as Moses did. In a type of vision called in the King James Bible a similitude, referred to in the book of Numbers chapter 12 v 8 when the Lord speaks of Moses; *With him will I speak face to face, and not in riddles, and the similitude of the Lord shall he behold.* Similitude means a likeness, we know that because Moses saw the Lord face to face, he had to cover his face when he left His presence, so that the children of Israel should not see the reflected glory of the Lord on Moses' face. God spoke to Moses' mouth to mouth, not in riddles or parables, but clearly, so there was always clarity in their conversations.

VISIONS

Visions come to us when we are awake, often resting before the Lord. Many people experience more than one vision, and on more than one occasion. At the end of a vision we invariably end in praise and worship of the Lord. Again there are many examples in the scriptures of those who had visions and it is worth looking at some of them.

Isaiah has a vision that is recorded in the book of Isaiah chapter 6. Here we are shown clearly the process a vision may follow. V1 *In the year King Uzziah died, I saw the Lord seated on throne, high and exalted, and the train of His robe filled the temple.* We see here a clear recollection of the time and place of the vision. V2 *Above Him were seraphs, each with six wings ; With two they covered their faces, with two they covered their feet, and with two they were flying.* Here is a clear recollection of physical images seen in the vision. V3 *And they were calling to one another; Holy, Holy, Holy is the Lord Almighty; the whole earth is filled with His glory.* When a vision is received the holiness of God is perceived. V4 *At the sound of their voices the door posts and thresholds shook and the temple was filled with smoke.* The awesomeness is very evident when God speaks. V5 *Woe to me I cried I'm ruined ! For I am a man of unclean lips, and live among a people of unclean lips, and my eyes have seen the King, the Lord Almighty.* When faced with the Holiness of God our own sinfulness becomes apparent and we cry out to God in our sin and shame.

Isaiah remembers clearly when he had the vision, and what he saw even though the book of Isaiah was written many years later, he has a perfect recall as to what happened to him. He says in the year King

Uzziah died I had a vision. He then describes what he heard in the heavenly realm. The effect of what he experienced is clearly seen in V5. *He recognises his sin, and uncleanness before the Lord.* *"Woe is me",* he says *"I am ruined for I am a man of unclean lips and live among a people of unclean lips".* He saw his sinfulness and the sinfulness of the people of Israel when he saw the Holiness of God, as His glory filled the temple.

SIN

His sin was taken away as the seraph touched his lips with hot coals. Our sin has also been taken away if we have accepted Jesus Christ as our Saviour—Messiah and have been cleansed with His blood which was shed on the Cross of Calvary where He was crucified and made a sacrifice to pay the price instead of us. His blood was shed as an atonement for our sins, mine and yours. No longer is there a need for bulls and goats to be sacrificed. The Lamb of God has paid the price for our sins once and for all, the perfect sacrifice, God the Father gave, to redeem us from our sin.

Faced with the presence of the Lord in a vision we are convicted of our unrighteousness and our desperate need of Him. Cleansed from our sin we can enter the Holy of Holies and come into our Heavenly Father's presence. Here in the Lord's presence Isaiah heard the Lord God speak these words recorded in Isaiah chapter 6 v 8; *Whom shall I send and who will go for us?* The commissioning must always come from the Father. He alone can send us out to do His work. Jesus reminds us in the Gospel of John chapter 17 v 4 and John 14 v 31 that he has brought glory to the Father by completing the works He had given Him to do. If Jesus had to do exactly what the Father commanded, how much more must we also be obedient and do the works the Lord has planned for us.

BOOK OF LIFE

Recently I heard of an African pastor who went to heaven for several days. While he was there he saw the Book of Life. He said that on each page was the name of a believer and below his or her name was a list of works each person had been designated to do since before time began. In the book of Ephesians chapter 2 v 10. *For we are God's workmanship, created in Christ Jesus to do good works, which God prepared in advance for us to do.* This scripture confirms what the Pastor saw.

Visions were given to Daniel, Ezekiel and Peter to name but a few. However, it is in the book of Habakkuk we discover how to respond to a vision from the Lord.

Habakkuk chapter 2 v 1 tells us, *Though the vision tarry, wait for it.* In other words, pray and seek the Lord, wait on the Lord and listen to what He has to say. V2 suggests that we write it down. *To take our stand and write down what the Lord says.* It helps in the days when doubt assails us to have the vision written down, to remind us of His plans and purposes for us, and it will come into being. Verse 3 says; Don't give up! Keep praying: Though it tarry wait for it. Remember the examples we have in scripture of those who have gone before us, but failed to wait God's appointed time.

ABRAHAM AND SARAH

In Abraham and Sarah we have an example of going before the Lord, not waiting for His perfect timing. In Genesis chapter 15 v 1-6 God reveals to Abraham that he will not remain childless, but will indeed father a son. Abraham believed God and it was credited to him as righteousness. Our heavenly Father is delighted when we receive His visions in faith, believing that He who spoke it will bring it into being. Ten years later after God had promised Abraham and Sarah a child, they were still childless.

Sarah decided that the only answer was for Abraham to have a child by her maid Hagar. In the culture that Abraham and Sarah lived in, this was not an unusual answer to their problem, if a wife gave a maid to her husband any children of the union were considered to belong to the mistress of the house, in this case, Sarah.

HAGAR

Hagar conceived and Ishmael was born. What Sarah thought was the answer to the problem became an even bigger problem as Hagar began to despise her mistress. Eventually, running away until God sent her back to Sarah God told Hagar, through an angel, to submit to Sarah. In addition, he told her that her son was to be named Ishmael and that he would be the first of many descendants too many to count. Ishmael was destined to become the first of what were to become the Arab nations. Abraham was eighty-six years of age when Ishmael was born.

Once again when Abraham was ninety—nine years of age the Lord appeared to him again, and told him Sarah would bear his child. Abraham did what so many of us have done when the Lord gives us a revelation, he laughed! In Genesis chapter 17 v17, it tells us Abraham fell face down; he laughed and said to himself, *Will a son be born to a man a hundred years old? Will Sarah bear a child at the age of ninety?* Sarah too laughed when she heard the three men visiting their tent say that *by this time next year Sarah would give birth to a son* (Genesis chapter 18 v10).

When we are passed the stage were we can't do anything about bringing into being our vision, God steps in and performs a miracle. It is only when we come to the end of ourselves can the Lord accomplish His plans through us.

Abraham was one hundred years old and Sarah ninety, long past the age of bearing children even accounting for the differences in length of life and child bearing years, but God is able.

Later in the book of Genesis chapter 21v1- 3 we see that Issac was indeed born to Sarah and Abraham, and he was named appropriately Issac, meaning he laughs.

ISHMAEL

The birth of Ishmael only produced anguish and pain for Sarah, having done things her own way. When we try to bring about the accomplishment of God's plans in our own strength it all goes wrong ultimately. It may seem good, but it is not the best way. God's way is always the best way. Three years later Ishmael and his mother had to be sent out of the camp of Abraham and Sarah to live in the wilderness, as Ishmael's obvious dislike and resentment toward Isaac began to surface. However, the Lord had a plan and purpose for Ishmael, this is recorded in Genesis chapter 21 v 11-21. The matter distressed Abraham greatly because it concerned his son. However, God said to him: *Do not be distressed about the boy and your maidservant. Listen to whatever Sarah tells you, because it is through Isaac that your offspring will be reckoned. I will make the son of the maidservant into a nation also, because he is your offspring.* Here we see the birth of the Arab nation, Ishmael was to be its founder member. While Isaac was the founder of the Jewish people.

From this one man Abraham, two nations were born, only to be at war with each other throughout history.

The consequences of our own actions can have far reaching implications for the future, sometimes effecting the Lord's plans for us. Like Sarah, I too had my own solutions to bringing into being the vision the Lord had given me.

CHAPTER 7

When the Lord gives us a revelation of any kind, it brings with it responsibility, and for that we need to be prepared. If we are willing to co-operate with Him, the Lord will train us up for those responsibilities.

One of the first lessons we need to learn, is dying to self. How this flesh of ours gets in the way, and frequently will not lie down, hindering what the Lord desires to do in our lives.

Jesus said in John chapter 12 v 24; *Unless a grain of wheat falls into the ground and dies it remains alone, but if it dies it bears much fruit.* In order that we bear much fruit for the kingdom, we need to die to ourselves and live for Christ. So often in this life we do what seems good, rather than what the Lord has prepared for us.

WOOD STUBBLE AND HAY

The result, is *wood, stubble and hay.* We should have been producing gold, silver and precious jewels as described in 1 Corinthians chapter 3 v 12-13. It tells us that *wood, stubble and hay will all be burnt up in the last day, only the gold, silver and precious jewels will remain.* These precious materials are the product of accomplishing that which the Lord has planned and purposed. While the wood, stubble and hay are the result of doing our own works, good as they may seem, even needed by the church or community, it may not necessarily be what the Lord had planned for us. There can be a lot of time and energy wasted amongst God's people, simply because we fail to come into the Lord's plans, often not even bothering to stop and check with Him if this is what he requires of us.

JOSEPH IN A PIT

Joseph was prepared by God to govern Egypt. When we look at his life we begin to realise that every apparent negative turn of events in his life led to him being given increasing amounts of responsibility. When Joseph was seventeen years of age he was taken into captivity. By the time he was thirty, fourteen years later, he was fully trained to be the right hand man of Pharaoh, ruler of Egypt. How did that happen?

When Joseph was originally taken into captivity, he was bought as a slave and sold on to Potiphar, who was one of Pharaoh's officials. Joseph ran Potiphar's household, no mean feat for a seventeen year old.

POTIPHAR'S WIFE

Later Joseph was wrongly accused by Potiphar's wife, and was put in prison, only to find himself with more responsibility. This time he is to be responsible for all those in the prison. This story is recorded in the book of Genesis in chapter 39; it tells us that Joseph's master took him and put him in prison, the place where the king's prisoners were confined. But while Joseph was there in the prison, the Lord was with him, he showed him kindness and granted him favour in the eyes of the prison warden. So the warden put Joseph in charge of all those in the prison, and he was made responsible for all that was done there. The warden paid no attention to anything under Joseph's care, the Lord was with Joseph and gave him success in whatever he did. Each time Joseph found himself in adverse conditions the Lord blessed him and prospered him. He was attacked and abandoned by his brothers and Potiphar's wife seduced him and wrongly accused him, but none of these things were ever able to separate Joseph from the love of God. God takes all our circumstances and uses them to

His praise and glory.

PRISON

As we read through the account of Joseph's life in prison, we begin to see his concern for others developing. Joseph, as a young boy, came across as uncaring of other people's feelings and very self-centred. Now we find the Lord developing a caring personality, someone who could see that other people had feelings and problems. In Genesis chapter 40 v 6 it tells us that Joseph noticed the cup bearer and baker were looking dejected. The once uncaring Joseph would have ridiculed these men, now he stops and talks to them, seeking to find out why they are so cast down. They share with him the dreams they both have had and explained that there was no one to interpret these dreams. The old Joseph would have pushed himself forward immediately. However, God is making changes to Joseph's character; he no longer rushes in, instead he asks the men if they believe that interpretations belong to God. When they confirm their belief in God's ability, Joseph offers to seek the Lord regarding their dreams. So Joseph is able to interpret their dreams. He is able to tell the cup bearer he is to be released from prison, and put back into service for his master—Pharaoh the King. The baker wasn't so fortunate for he was to be hung within three days. Joseph's interpretations were proved to be correct.

CUP BEARER

When the cup bearer was released from prison Joseph had asked the cup bearer to speak to the Pharaoh on his behalf, explaining that he had been wrongly imprisoned. It was to be two more years before the cup bearer was to remember Joseph's request. Pharaoh himself begins to have dreams; then the cup bearer remembers Joseph in prison. Maybe Joseph began to despair of ever getting out of prison. I don't think so. We too can begin to feel that the Lord, having given us some revelation of His plans for us, has promptly forgotten us. Again, that wouldn't be true, He never forgets, He is just preparing us. It is necessary to develop patience, if we are to be equipped, to do the Lord's work.

RELEASE

Finally Joseph is called from prison, his time of preparation is nearly over. Almost fourteen years have passed since Joseph was so cruelly thrown into that pit by his brothers, Did Joseph rush from his prison cell looking like a man who had been incarcerated many years? No! The Bible tells us that when he had shaved and changed his clothing, he came before Pharaoh. Joseph didn't come before him as a prisoner, but as an ambassador of the Lord. He looked the part of a future government official. There was no sign of any loss of faith on Joseph's part, in fact humility had replaced the old brashness, for when Pharaoh asks if he can interpret the dream he clearly states that he can't interpret his dream but God could. Pharaoh tells Joseph about the dreams he has had, and the Lord tells Joseph what the dreams mean. Egypt is going to experience seven years of mighty crops followed by seven years of famine. This was not only going to affect Egypt, but neighbouring countries as well.

Fourteen years of managing households and prisons have equipped Joseph in just the manner Egypt's government needed, to plan and prepare for the coming years if Egypt is to survive the famine of the coming years. Joseph is able to point out these needs to Pharaoh convincing him that Joseph was just the man he needed to head up this project. Joseph is set free to serve the Lord and Egypt in the capacity the Lord had planned before time began for Joseph.

PROMOTION

Joseph now finds himself second in command to Pharaoh, in charge of the palace and all Pharaoh's people. What a promotion, from prison to palace. Only the Lord can bring this about. Pharaoh gave Joseph his ring of authority and dressed him in fine linen.

When we are released into the Lord's service, we too are given the ring of authority, that is to use the name of Jesus. We are told by Jesus himself, that whatever we ask in His name, He will do it, that the Father may be glorified in the Son (John chapter 14 vs 13- 14).

The disciples reported to Jesus that even the demons left when they used his name. They were using the authority given to them, that is the name of Jesus.

DISAPPOINTMENT

Many people are disappointed when they ask for things in Jesus' name when they don't receive what they ask for. One reason for this can be due to our lack of relationship with the Lord; we can't expect to receive from the Lord if we are not in a relationship with Him. It is easy to fall into the 'ask and expect mode' becoming disappointed when we don't receive. We can also ask and not ask in accordance with the Lord's desire, therefore not receiving.

Joseph also received robes of fine linen. We too, as the Lord's children receive a robe of fine linen: this is described in Revelation chapter 19 v 8 where it states we will receive a white linen robe bright and clean, to wear. Fine linen stands for the righteous acts of the saints.

JACOB

Eventually the famine affects neighbouring Canaan. Jacob, Joseph's father sends his sons to Egypt to buy food where eventually after two years of Joseph testing his brothers he is reconciled to them and meets his father again. Joseph's dreams are fulfilled for his father and his brothers bow down to him just as he had seen. Indeed, his sheaves where bigger than those of his brothers. He had risen from being a shepherd boy, being put in prison, to becoming second in command to Egypt's top man.

So our dreams and visions given by the Lord will come to pass if we wait patiently and co-operate with the Lord. The potter has to make the clay into the vessel that is necessary to fulfil its required function. We need to let the Lord melt us and mould us into that which is needed to come into His plans and purposes.

JESUS PREPARED

Jesus also had to be prepared for His ministry. For thirty years He was hidden away developing the skills of life, in addition to developing his carpentry skills. He no doubt used to earn a living before it was His time to be released into His Father's plan and purpose for Him. Luke records something of the preparation Jesus underwent. When he went into the wilderness it was so that He might be tested by the devil. When we talk about going through the wilderness, it is often because we have become slack in our walk with the Lord, we fail to pray and read the scriptures as we should, then we wonder why we are weak and our lives are barren and fruitless. Unless we remain in the vine, the spirit of the Lord cannot flow through us. We must remain close to Jesus if we are to grow and flourish.

THE WILDERNESS

The three areas Satan tempted Jesus are the three areas most prevalent in our lives. Food, Authority and Worship.

Jesus was in the wilderness for forty days and nights before Satan started to tempt Him. The wilderness is a very beautiful place, an awesome place, with a real sense of the power of God . Miles and miles of barren hills and valleys, empty wadis, an occasional bush or tree, very weak- looking clumps of vegetation, usually indicating that there is a supply of water hidden under ground. Despite the beauty and grandeur of the scenery, it is no place to be caught up in battle with the enemy, even if you are the Son of God. Jesus was there battling as the Son of Man. It was in His humanity He battled with the enemy of our souls, not as the Son of God using His kingly power. However, in the wilderness as on the cross, He defeated the enemy as the Son of Man, as a human being not in His Godly power and authority.

If at any time in the wilderness Jesus had called upon His heavenly authority, He would have ceased to be the perfect sacrifice, and therefore unable to take our sin upon Himself on the cross and pay the price for our salvation.

TEMPTATION

Jesus had gone forty days without food before Satan started tempting Him. Then, knowing Jesus would be physically hungry Satan said, If you are the Son of God, command these stones to become bread. For Jesus, as for any one of us, this would be a temptation as Jesus by now would be extremely hungry. However, Jesus responds by telling Satan, Man does not live by bread alone. Jesus was telling Satan, I know where to get my bread, meaning spiritual food, for He knew the scriptures, the continuation of this quotation being, that man lives by every word that proceeds from the mouth of God (Deuteronomy chapter 8 v 3).

The next temptation Jesus experienced was on the grounds of authority. *The devil took Jesus to a high place and showed him in an instant, all the kingdoms of the world, and he said to him I will give you all their authority and splendour, for it has been given to me, and I can give it to anyone I want to. So if you worship me it will be all yours.* Satan wanted Jesus to bow down and worship, and serve only him so he offered Him the world. This is Satan the fallen tarnished angel offering Jesus the King of glory, false glory. Jesus response again came from scripture; this time from Deuteronomy chapter 6 v 13; *It is written; Worship the Lord your God and serve Him only.*

Again Satan tempts Jesus by taking Him to Jerusalem. Many believe Satan took Jesus to the pinnacle of the temple overlooking the Kidron Valley in Jerusalem. Traditionally when blood was shed for the sacrifice for sin it flowed down into the Kidron Valley. Satan was indicating to Jesus that he knew Jesus was intended to become the sacrifice for sin for the whole world and that His blood would flow, so that we might be cleansed from our sin, healed and restored. Scripture is quoted again, this time by Satan. In Luke chapter 4 where this incident is recorded in v 9

IF YOU ARE THE SON OF GOD

The devil lead Jesus to Jerusalem and had him stand on the highest point of the temple. *If you are the Son of God he said throw yourself down from here. For it is written He will command angels concerning you to guard you carefully; they will lift you up in their hands, so that you will not strike your foot against a stone.* Jesus answered *It says: Do not put the Lord your God to the test.* Satan attempts to persuade Jesus that God will not allow Jesus to be hurt, but will send His angels to help Him. Jesus response is to state quite clearly we should not test the Lord our God. After this we are told Satan left Jesus until a more opportune time, meaning when He was on the cross, all alone without the love and power of God the Father to support Him.

We too will be tempted , and we can be sure that Satan will tempt us in the same areas Jesus was tempted in. Satan is always looking for ways to get us to bow down to him. He deceives us frequently in the area of worship, many in the church today, sing praises to each other or even themselves, rather than to the Lord. Often our worship is sadly, of the flesh or the world, both of which are governed by the enemy of our souls.

MANY WILL SAY

Who has the authority in your life? Is it Jesus or have we taken it back again, leaving the enemy an open door. Jesus said that in the last days. *Many will say to me on that day Lord, Lord did we not prophesy in your name, and in your name drive out demons and perform many miracles? Then I will tell them plainly I never knew you, away from me you evil doer.*

Spiritual food is vitally important if we are to stand against the wiles of the enemy. Look how Jesus told Satan, that man does not live by bread alone, but by every word that proceeds from the mouth of God. Sadly I meet too many Christians who are ministering in the name of Jesus, but who only read their Bible two or three times a week. How would you feel if you only ate food two or three times a week? Very weak you can be sure. That is how it is spiritually if we only read the word of God occasionally. How can we expect to stand in the day of trouble?

ON OUR HEARTS

The word of the Lord needs to be written on our hearts. Jesus knew the scriptures and when Satan tried to deceive Him by misquoting scripture, Jesus was able to put him right. If a preacher misquotes the scriptures, do you know, are you aware? Can you quote scripture at the enemy when he attacks you? We must in these days, store the word in our hearts because, when persecution comes, we will need to be able to comfort ourselves with the word of the Lord. In countries where Christians are persecuted for their faith, their Bibles are inevitably destroyed. How do they survive? It is by knowing the word of the Lord.

During the years the Lord has been preparing me I have been challenged in similar areas to Jesus, and in another chapter of this book I will share some of my testings. Testings, that I did not always come out of as well as our Lord Jesus Christ, who was tested in His humanity, just as we are. He overcame the enemy, but we are not always that victorious.

Some years previously the Lord had shown me that when I married again I would not have a long courtship.

JIM

Jim had been backslidden when I met him. He said he had known Jesus in his teenage years, but had fallen away some years later. He started to come to church with me and when conversations turned to baptism by immersion, He said he had not been baptised, having been in a denomination that did not recognise the need for baptism. He decided he wanted to be baptised and some weeks later this took place. Naturally, I was delighted for baptism is always, or should be, a special occasion in a believer's life.

When Jim asked me to marry him, I had no hesitation in acccepting. We asked the elders of the fellowship for their blessing, not knowing what their response would be, as we fellowshipped in a denomination that did not believe in marrying those who had previously been divorced. The elders prayed about it and to our delight agreed. One elder said his initial reaction had been, that this marriage was not acceptable. He told us that the Lord had rebuked him, by saying; *How dare you call unclean, that which I have called clean!* With that he agreed with his fellow elder. Seeing this as approval from the Lord, we went ahead and arranged the wedding with a reception to follow.

A REAL FRIEND

Pat is a Christian friend who worked with me. Three days before the wedding, she came to visit me at my home. She came to tell me that she felt the Lord was saying I didn't have to marry Jim if I didn't want to. What an odd statement I thought, but I knew it had not been easy for Pat to come and say what she had. I also knew how she loved the Lord and me, and would only share this with me after much prayer. What should I do? I prayed and sought the Lord, but could not perceive anything further, the key had to be "I didn't have to marry him if I didn't want too!" Well of course I wanted to marry Jim, I loved him and he loved me, didn't he? In the fulness of time I came to know why the Lord was giving me the opportunity to opt out, for I was marrying an angel of light, as I was soon to discover.

CHAPTER 8

Coming into Gods plans and purposes is a process, and that process has many parts to it—each part inevitably takes time. We are often told that if something is of the Lord it will happen quickly, this is not necessarily true. There is a lot of preparation needed before most of us are ready to move into what the Lord has for us, particularly if this is our first major exploit with the Lord. Later when we have undertaken several major tasks for the Lord less preparation will be needed. However, there is a constant need to die to self if we are to serve the Lord. Frequently we will find ourselves in circumstances that will stretch us in our walk with the Lord. Daily taking up our cross is essential for each of as we are called to serve the Lord. However we all have a tendency to forget much of what the Lord has trained us in , so there will be times when we will need to relearn some of the things the Lord has previously taught us.

REVELATION

In the beginning there has to be a revelation from the Lord. That revelation has to be checked against the word of the Lord, the Bible. Each of us has our own way of checking revelations out, but the Bible tells us the Lord reveals His word to us, then again to confirm it.

Birthing a vision or revelation is the next step. What do we mean by birthing it? Prayer is the key, praying into it, pray without ceasing, until the Lord reveals to you that it is ratified in heaven. This part of the process can take months or years. I spent three continuous years praying into this particular vision I am sharing with you in this book. Sometimes we will hear the Lord saying it is ratified in heaven, now bring it down to earth, as I did. Other times we may sense in our spirit that the time to pray into the vision or revelation is over, and the project will come to pass.

A FLEECE

Gideon used a fleece to confirm the outcome of his request. If we look at the book of Judges chapter 6 vs 36-40, we find Gideon saying to God; *If you will save Israel by my hand, as you have promised, look, I will place a wool fleece on the threshing floor. If there is dew only on the fleece and all the ground is dry, then I will know you will save Israel by my hand, as you said.* So that is what happened. Gideon rose early the next day he squeezed the fleece and wrung out the dew a bowl full of water. Then Gideon said; *do not be angry with me. Let me make just one more request. Allow me one more test with the fleece make the fleece dry and the ground covered with dew. That night God did so. Only the fleece was dry, all the ground was covered with dew.* Here we see how God confirmed twice to Gideon that it was His will that Gideon would be used to rescue Israel. However in this instance God was angry with Gideon that he laid out the fleece because He had previously told Gideon that He was going to use him. Gideon acknowledges this as he refers to how the Lord is going to use him in these verses. From this example we can see that even when we display a lack of faith, He still blesses us.

SPELLING IT OUT

We can still learn how to ask the Lord for confirmation. Gideon made clear and specific requests of the Lord. He spelled out what he needed to see as a clear answer from the Lord. God is not a God of vagueness. He will tell us clearly what we need to know, when we need to know it. If you read on further in the book of Judges how the Lord leads Gideon, the Lord does it little by little, a step at a time. He knows we can't take in information in big chunks, but only in bite size portions. The Lord rarely shows us all of the big picture, because he knows we could not cope with that. Most of us would not be able to remember many of the specific instructions. Given time we would have forgotten most of what He had shared with us.

TIME SCALES

This incident with Gideon shows us something else to remember when we are seeking the Lord with requests, that is, remember to include time scales. These are important. How many works of the Lord have had to be aborted because we have got the timing wrong? A great many I fear. Timing is all important, Gideon didn't say to the Lord, when you feel ready just do as I have requested. No, he was specific, Gideon got up the next day expecting an answer from the Lord, and he got an answer. We can see from the pattern laid down that God responds to specific requests. Seeking the Lord in this way can be helpful when we are not used to making requests of the Lord. As we grow in faith we will not use this method too often because as we develop a relationship with the Father we will hear His voice more clearly as we seek to walk with Him.

LISTENING

Later on in the book of Judges we can see how the Lord spoke to Gideon as he learned to listen to the voice of the Lord, as his confidence in his ability to recognise the Lord's voice grew, so the Lord began to speak to him in a variety of ways.

THE KEY

Preparation is another key to being made ready for the task allotted to us. When we look how long it took the Lord to prepare Moses, David, Joseph and others we should not be surprised at the length of time it takes to prepare us. If we are going to be able to carry out the Lord's plans, in His way, we first of all have to learn His ways. It took the Lord fourteen years to prepare Joseph. With Moses it took forty years, despite the fact that Moses had been brought up in Pharaoh's household , and consequently would have been, quite well educated. Though education or Bible college training are not necessarily God's way of preparing a person. Moses having been well educated spent forty years in the back of the desert minding sheep. This was not considered by the Egyptians to be the sort of work an educated man should do. God started by humbling Moses he gave him a task to do that those much lower than himself on the social scale would have carried out.

IT SOMETIME SEEMS SENSELESS

Another thing the Lord knows is that if you are going to be used to move people around the desert for forty years you have to have some experience; not only of the desert and the ways of the desert, but the weather patterns, to say nothing of keeping wandering groups of sheep together. In the desert is the place to start hearing God's voice clearly. Learning to follow instruction and how to keep close to the Lord all takes time, it doesn't just happen over night. We can't pick it up by using other people's experience, though that is helpful and can guide us, but it only gives us head knowledge, this is of no real value in knowing the Lord, it is only by putting into practise what we see Moses and others doing that we begin to move with the Lord.

GOD DOES IT

How then do we bring these revelations into being? We don't, God does. It is sad, but true, that each one of us have probably spent time and energy on works that did not originate with Jesus Christ and on that final day when all works will be revealed for what they are, we will recognise that. Those works that are at His bidding will survive and come forth as gold, silver and precious stones and used to embroider our wedding gown at the marriage of the Lamb of God to his bride. What can we do about those works that we know are not from Him? Repent, ask for forgiveness, then forget them. Determine that in future you will only do what the Lord reveals to you and await His timing.

CHAPTER 9

When the Lord called me to be an intercessor, I was eight months pregnant with my daughter and it had been a difficult year. Charles, one of my brothers, had been killed in a freak accident at the beginning of the year. Two months later my Dad had died, having been rendered unconscious through a stroke for several weeks prior to his death. Following this, I discovered my first husband had become involved with a woman he worked with.

CALLED

It was in June that year that the Lord had called me to be an intercessor. I didn't know what an intercessor was. I just said "Yes Lord". Over the next twenty one years I was not allowed to tell any one of my calling as an intercessor. Frequently I would cry out to the Lord asking, "Why are things going wrong in my life?" For fourteen years the Lord took me through the life of Job. I lost almost everything. This was followed by seven years of testing in the wilderness. I had no one to check progress with, but along with my Bible and a copy of Rees Howells, 'Intercessor,' I ploughed a lonely furrow.

ORDINARY FAMILIES

My intercession started with situations that ordinary families had to cope with in the world today. These included money shortages, adultery, teenage rebellion, physical and sexual abuse, divorce, children being born outside of marriage, children living together without being married, and many more incidents which will not be shared within the pages of this book. Learning to cope with the trauma that these life experiences bring wasn't enough. Victory had to be gained. Forgiveness, love and acceptance of people had to be manifest as part of the outcome of each situation. Through God's grace I started to become an overcomer in each one of these situations that I had to live through, whilst supporting others in their needs. This ultimatley led to standing with Church leaders faced with various threats to their ministry and helping them to stand firm and overcome.

OVERCOMING

Money was in such short supply that I bought clothes at jumble sales and remade them into clothes for the family. I believe that as we do our bit to help in these financially constrained times, God will do His. Trusting in His financial provision does not mean we sit back and do nothing. We must play our part, take a little job, make the family's clothes or growing our own food all contributes to God's provision for us, as He has promised in His word to bless the work of our hands. However, I have been blessed in seeing the Lord provide financially in so many different ways, including increasing actual money.

A MIRACLE

It was late July and I knew that the next month was the month of the annual bills. My husband had been on strike for many months and this year money was in even shorter supply than usual. As I cried out to the Lord I heard the Lord say, "Put your husband's pay packet into the zipper pocket of your shopping bag, every time you need to pay a bill just put your hand in the pocket and take out what you need." I wondered at the validity of what I believed the Lord had said to me. Into my mind came a story from the Bible, so I looked it up. 2 Kings chapter 4 v 1-7 tells us of an incident that the prophet Elisha was involved in. One of the company of prophets had died leaving his widow with two sons. These sons would normally have helped the widow by working and taking their father's place, supporting her at her time of need. However the prophet had incurred debts during his time in office and now the creditors were planning to take the boys into slavery, to pay off their father,s debts. What would the poor widow do then? She had no money, no food and now her only means of support were being taken from her. She approached the prophet Elisha who said; "How can I help? Tell me what do you have in your house?" "Your servant has nothing there at all", she said "except a little oil". Elisha said, "Go around and ask all your neighbours for empty jars. Don't ask for just a few. Then go inside, and shut the door behind you and your sons. Pour oil into all the jars, and as each is filled, put it to one side."

The widow did as she was told and filled every bottle she could find, the little oil she had set off with kept flowing and flowing until every container was filled. *"Bring me another jar" she said , but he replied "there is not a jar left." She went and told the man of God and he said, "Go and sell the oil and pay your debts. You and your sons can live on what is left."*

That was how the Lord increased what little we had, and made enough out of it to pay all the bills that came in that month. I counted how much we had paid out of that small sum of money and found we had paid several hundred pounds in excess of that which had been placed in the pocket originally and there was even a little left over to buy me a dress to wear at a wedding we had been invited too.

WHAT IS AN INTERCESSOR?

What is an intercessor? According to the Bible it is one who stands in the gap. In the book of (Isaiah chapter 59 v 16) (King James Bible) *He saw that there was no man, and wondered that there was no intercessor.* This is one of just a few verses in the Bible that speaks about intercession.

Abraham interceded for the people of Sodom. He pleads with the Lord not to destroy Sodom. He cries out to the Lord to save the city. Abraham starts by saying *Lord if there are only fifty righteous people will you save the city?* Eventually he asks the Lord if there are only ten righteous people will He save the city. The Lord says He will save Sodom if there are only ten righteous people. However, as the story unfolds we find there is only Lot, his wife and daughters who are considered righteous. The Lord saved them, before He destroyed Sodom and Gomorrah. Abraham stood in the gap and pleaded for the people.

SOLOMON

Solomon interceded for the people of Israel. In 2 Chronicles chapter 6 Solomon prays a mighty pray, on several occasions he asks the Lord to forgive the people of Israel when they sin. His intercession covered the sins of the people in there various forms asking the Lord always to hear despite their sin. Ezra and Daniel also stood in the gap for the sins of the people.

Our greatest intercessor is the Lord Jesus himself. In the first epistle of John chapter 2 v 1 it states; *My dear children I write this to you so that you will not sin. But if anybody does sin, we have one who speaks to the Father in our defence—Jesus Christ the Righteous One.* Jesus is ever before the throne of God pleading on our behalf.

HOLY SPIRIT

The book of Hebrews chapter seven v 25 says; *Therefore he is able to save completely those who come to God through him, because he always lives to intercede for them.* Jesus is our intercessor. The Holy Spirit is also an intercessor. Those familiar verses in the book of Romans chapter eight vs 26 & 27; *In the same way, the Spirit helps us in our weakness. We do not know what we ought to pray for, but the Spirit himself intercedes for us with groans that words cannot express. And he who searches our hearts knows the mind of the Spirit, because the Spirit intercedes for the saints in accordance with the will of God.* However, when we don't know how to pray, or what to pray the Holy Spirit will intercede on our behalf.

In the first letter of Timothy, chapter two V1 it shows us that there is a difference between, requests, prayers and intercession. There has been much confusion in the church regarding intercession. Many teach intercession is prayer, but in this verse it shows us that there is more to this than prayer. For the writer, Paul differentiates between the two, indicating that there is more to intercession than just prayer.

Rees Howells the well known intercessor was used by God to stand in the gap for many lost souls, he would pray for days, going without food in order that his intercession might be more effective. Intercessors are called to fulfil the role the Lord has planned and purposed for them. It is a calling that is usually carried out in secret before the throne of God.

CHAPTER 10

For fourteen years, I had lived the life of Job. Every time I cried out to the Lord He would remind me of Job and all he lost and yet he still worshipped the Lord. Job lost his family, home, wealth and his marriage was a joke, but he still refused to curse God.

I too lost almost everything. "Lay your home and family on the altar," the Lord said to me one day, so I did. Before many years were completed, I came to a point where, but for the grace of God and his intervention, I would have lost it all.

UCB

The daily study notes of United Christian Broadcasting are often a great blessing to me. The Lord uses them in my life in many different ways. Here's a gem from one of their recent readings that encapsulates what it means to lay everything on the altar. "Before you find life's purpose, you often go through a series of adversities that cause you to let go of the temporal and grasp the eternal! For Paul that meant the loss of everything. We see this recorded in the letter to the Philippians chapter 3 v 8; What is more, I consider everything of loss compared to the surpassing greatness of knowing Christ Jesus my Lord, for whose sake I have lost all things. I consider them rubbish, that I may gain Christ. For others, it means the 'heat of battle' in a divorce court when the one person they thought was 'everything' walks away and they're suddenly stripped down to what they had before. Look at Job; his home is a shambles, his marriage is a joke, and his children are dead. That's when he discovered that you can be stripped only of the temporal, but not the eternal: stripped of wealth, friends, and fame, but not character, class or Christ, they survive the strippings of life!

Listen, Then Job fell down upon the ground and worshipped. Job chapter 1 v 20. Worship is born when real sacrifice occurs. When we lay on the altar something you thought you had to have, because you now realise it was God's all the time, that's worship. Look at Abraham's altar in Genesis chapter 22 v 2; Then God said, Take your son , your only son, Isaac, whom you love, and go to the region of Moriah. Sacrifice him there as a burnt offering on one of the mountains I will tell you about. God didn't want the slain body of Isaac, He only wanted to know Is there anything you love more than me? That's it, reaching the place where you can pray: "Lord here are my grudges and my unforgiveness. Here's my need to impress. Here's my time and my overtime. Here's anything I'm wrapped up in that hinders me from being completely Yours. You'll never have to take these things from me, for I gladly give You all it takes to be what You want me to be."

THE ENEMY CREATES HAVOC

These words came to me nearly twenty years after my reputation was gone. I was a deacon in the church when my first marriage ended. I was asked to resign. It was supposedly because I was involved with evangelism in the community. It was said it would be better to step down as I would no longer have as much time to work in the church! That hurt because it came immediately after my divorce. I was feeling particularly vulnerable and, at the very time when I needed support, I was receiving the reverse. I praise the Lord that he kept me walking with him in the face of the discouragement. Sometimes Satan is allowed to come and create havoc in our lives for a season. In the book of Job chapter 1 v 6-12 we find Satan coming before God; Where have you come from" God asks him. from roaming through the earth and going back and forth in it Satan replies, God replies by asking Satan if he has considered his servant Job, The Lord's appraisal of Job was that there was no one like him in all the earth, a man who was blameless, upright and shunned evil. Satan replies by pointing out Job has cause to fear God, particularly as God has built a hedge around him and all that he has, Satan continues, v10; Have you not put a hedge around him and his household and everything he has? You have blessed the work of his hands, so that his flocks and herds are spread throughout the land. But stretch out your hand and strike everything he has, and he will surely curse you to your face. The Lord said to Satan; Very well, then, everything he has is in your hands, but on the man himself do not lay a finger. Job lost everything, In chapter two we find Satan is back from doing his worst to Jobs family and finances, the Lord said to Satan; see I told you he wouldn't curse me. Ha, said Satan, just let me get to the man. If I can get to him he will surely curse you. Alright said God, but you mustn't kill him. God knew his man, because despite all that Satan threw at Job, still he would not curse the Lord, so Satan retired defeated.

WORLDLY WISE

I first met Mrs Thomas when I became a warden in sheltered accommodation. She was a widow and had lived in the south of England since her marriage many years before. Now, in her seventies, she wanted to return to the area where she had lived in her youth. There had of course been a great many changes to the area since she had left more than fifty years previously.

She had heard of the flats available in our complex, and so it was arranged that she should visit the flats to see if she liked them. She was very impressed with the spaciousness of the flats and the comfort of the communal lounge. The residents made her very welcome, but there was one major problem, Tibby the cat. There was a ruling that didn't allow residents to keep cats or dogs. She was very upset, but she didn't want to part with her cat, so what could be done.

Mrs Thomas had made a journey of more than three hundred miles to visit the area, so it was important to try and find accommodation while she was in the area. Knowing the locality as I did, I knew that she may find herself being housed by the Local Authority in a less desirable part of the town, an area unsuitable for elderly people living on their own.

Then I remembered my house. The house was for sale, but empty, as we were living on site while I worked as a warden. She could borrow my house I thought. With hindsight this was not the best idea I had come up with! I was just about to discover that this sweet elderly lady knew her way around the world's systems better than I did.

I took her to visit the house and the area it was situated in. It was just off a main road near the shops and on the edge of the countryside and she loved it. It would be ideal she said while she looked around the town to find something else.

A CHALLENGE

On August the first she moved into the house, complete with Tibby the long haired white cat. Three weeks later on the eve of the holiday I was taking in France with two of my children, a strange thing happened, I received a letter! Not so strange you may say. However, there was a national postal strike on at the time. Why I looked in the mail box, I don't know, but there it was, a letter, hand delivered from a lawyer.

What a shock I received when I opened the letter and read the contents. Would you believe it, that dear old lady I loaned my house too, had gone and taken legal advice to see whether she could legally claim to be a squatter in my house and claim the house for herself.

Immediately, I telephoned my lawyer, explained the situation to her. She told me I was in a very serious situationas legally the lady could claim to be a squatter and take the house from me. To rub salt in my wounds I was told I would have to pay the mortgage. Wow, what a mess!

Then I remembered I had written Mrs Thomas a letter after I had agreed to lend her the house, in which I stated I was lending her the house for a period of three months, while she looked around for somewhere else to live. Why had I gone to the trouble to photocopy this letter? It was so out of character for me to do so, but I had kept a copy of the letter. The letter made all the difference: the legal people agreed, Mrs Thomas had known the terms of the agreement and could not claim squatters rights, so that was that. Next day I paid a visit to my lawyer, leaving the copy of the letter in her hands, then we set off on our holiday knowing it was all in the Lord's hands, and he would sort out the rest of the problem. Two months later Mrs Thomas and Tibby left for pastures new.

Placing the house on the altar had nearly cost me dearly, but not nearly as high a price as Abraham was willing to pay when the Lord asked him to put Isaac on the altar.

Following the pattern of Job's life meant losing everything, including some of those who called themselves friends.

SO CALLED FRIENDS

However, one friend was, and still is, very special—Linda. Linda and I spent ten years working together in a poor area of our hometown, working with children, running Bible based kid's clubs. Linda was single at the time, and was always there for me, listening to the latest happenings with loving patience, encouraging me to believe God was in control of my life and that He would work it out. Then one day she phoned me to say, that in the light of the latest' happening' she had been tempted to become a friend of Job, one of those who was no friend at all, but she went on to say, the Lord had spoken to her clearly stating that all these events that kept happening in my life, was because as with Job , Satan had been allowed to test me. How relieved we both were to know all that had been going on in my life, for so long was because the Lord allowed Satan to have his way for a season. Linda remains very precious to me, she has been married many years now and has four lovely children. How I praise the Lord for this friend, who stuck closer than a brother, and refused to become one of Job's famous friends to me.

CAST TO THE DEVIL

Many years later I discovered why I had under gone this severe challenging of so much in my life. Previously I had been a member of a Free Evangelical Church for around ten years. I loved the people and was blessed by the teaching though some of it fell short of the full Biblical truth. The gifts of the Holy Spirit were believed to have died out along with many other teachings to do with the Holy Spirit. Part of the Church constitution stated that you could never leave that particular fellowship, even if you went to live in Australia or else where in England. You could not leave the fellowship and become a member of another fellowship. I had moved to a nearby town, near enough to travel to the fellowship. However I felt the Lord through scripture calling me to a local Baptist Church, so I started to attend that fellowship. My previous Pastor came to hear of this and along with the elders approached my new Pastor, insisting that he order me to return to my former fellowship. This he refused to do believing as I did that we should worship in a local fellowship. The result of this is that the leaders of my old fellowship cast me to the devil in line with the scriptures in 1 Corinthians chapter 5. This chapter has nothing to do with moving Church rather it talks about adultery, but such was the interpretation of the scriptures at that time by this fellowship that they cast me to the devil, which caused me a lot of pain and sadness for many years.

Now the life of Job was behind me, the Lord told me to collect worship tapes because he was going to send me into the wilderness. I was to leave the lively fellowship I was part of and go into a traditional fellowship that did not move in the gifts of the spirit. My Pastor at the time agreed that this was what the Lord was saying to me. Little did I know what was waiting for me.

CHAPTER 11

John Bunyan in Pilgrim's Progress describes the Christian walk, as one where we regularly get side tracked down various pathways that tempt us along the way. In his book, he describes the adventures Pilgrim has upon the way. Many are called by names we would recognise. Vanity being one such name. He meets many characters. Pride and Timidity being but two. The reason I mention this book, is because each of us will meet red herrings, get side tracked along the path we are walking as we seek to come into the plans and purposes of the Lord. These will vary according to our nature, spiritual maturity and openness to the Lord.

WRONG TURNING

One of the wrong turnings I took while in pursuit of the house in my particular vision, was to go to a village I had lived in as a child. In this village I found a job with a nice detached house with it. I thought perhaps this is where the vision would come into being.

Great Eccleston is a lovely village in the heart of the English countryside. I had lived near there for a few years when I was a child. In adulthood the beauty of the area had often drawn me for a visit as it was only a one hour drive from the town I had moved to with my Mother, brothers and sister when our parent's marriage broke down many years before. Now I was considering moving back to the place of my childhood memories, but had I heard the Lord correctly?

HATS

How difficult it is sometimes to know what the Lord really means by what He is saying. I remember the time the Lord started to show me the scripture concerning women covering their heads. Paul talks about this in 1 Corinthians chapter 11 vs 3-10; Now I want you to realise that the head of every man is Christ, and the head of every woman is man, and the head of Christ is God. Every man who prays or prophesies with his head covered dishonours his head. And every woman who prays or prophesies with her head uncovered dishonours her head, it is just as though her head were shaved. If a woman does not cover her head, she should have her hair cut off, and if it is a disgrace for a woman to have her hair cut or shaved off, she should cover her head. When I saw this scripture I thought I should start wearing a hat to cover my head when I went to church. So this is what I started to do. Sometime later the Lord took me back to this scripture again, and showed me that what was really meant by this scripture. He said it was about the state of our heart. If our heart was right with God women didn't need to wear a hat, so I got my heart right with Him and started to go to church without a hat on my head. So much of the Christian life is encapsulated in this aspect of getting our hearts right with God. Much of what we have misguidedly seen to be the truth will, I believe be forgiven us on the final day. Because we have not erred deliberately we just have not seen the truth of the word as it was intended.

FOGGY DAYS

When I realised I was not clear as to what the Lord was really saying about the job I had applied for in the village of my childhood, I should have stopped and checked and waited until I was sure I had heard from Him, but I didn't.

I decided to carry on and apply for the vacancy that had occurred for a warden in sheltered accommodation in this village, the post had a detached house with it, maybe this was the house of the vision I had thought.

When the letter arrived inviting me to attend an interview, I was quite excited, I rang a friend and told her of the forthcoming interview, and she offered to come with me. On the appointed day we set off on our journey, apprehensive but excited. Was this going to be the day that I would begin to come into the vision? The interview went well I was confident I had given a good account of myself. Now we would just have to wait and see. The Lord was in control after all. A few days later I was informed that the job was mine did I want it? Was this really what the Lord wanted for me? A check in my spirit led me to pray further and more intensely. I felt in my spirit that the job offer was a 'good' move but it was not the best the Lord had for me, so I declined the offer. When I shared this with my Pastor, he too felt it would not have been the best the Lord had for me. Again the Lord confirmed His word. Many years later when I finally found the house the Lord had planned for me, I understood why when the Lord had referred to the location of the house I was to have, I had thought of my home village. I was looking with carnal eyes, not spiritual eyes. For the house that I was to receive had great spiritual meaning in its purpose, but of course I wasn't aware of that at this time.

The illustration of wearing a hat is a good example of this. We often think in terms of what we can see, in my case a hat. Instead of which the Lord thinks in terms of things of the spirit. The condition of our heart is more important to the Lord than what we wear on our head.

GOING WRONG AGAIN

Can or does the Lord use these apparent wrong turnings in our life? Yes He does, because nothing is wasted in the kingdom of God. Everything that happens to us, no matter how painful, is used by the Lord. Through writing this book the Lord has given me a glimpse of the front of the tapestry that our lives are producing and every thing that has ever happened to us is there, being used to make up the whole of the picture. When sewing a piece of embroidery we only concentrate on one area at a time. It is only when it is completed that we see the importance of the apparent bits that fill in the gaps to make the whole picture. When we appreciate the value of the apparently insignificant moments of our lives , do we come, to value every moment for what it is.

VISITING

During the period that I applied for the post of warden, the Lord spoke to me of a particular fellowship in a nearby town, located close to where the vacancy existed. On a Sunday evening I would drive fifty miles or so to this fellowship. The Lord had shown me, in a revelation, this fellowship. He told me the denomination and the road the building was located on. The first time I went to the fellowship was just before Easter. The Lord spoke to me about the fellowship and said He wanted to use me there. The next meeting was to be on Good Friday, there was to be a faith lunch afterwards. It seemed a good opportunity to get to know people, so I put my name down on the list as needing lunch the following Friday. On Good Friday morning I drove to the fellowship as planned. While waiting for the service to start, the Lord told me to bind the religious and traditional spirits in the place, and loose the Holy Spirit into the meeting. I was not in the habit of doing this at the time, but I did as the Lord said. When the service was over I was sat near the Pastor's wife and her friend, who together made up the worship group. She was saying to her friend. "Did you notice anything different this morning in church?" She went on to say to her friend, "For the first time I was able to think in the meeting and hear from God." We don't always realise that evil spirits , named religious and traditional spirits can hinder us from hearing from the Lord and keep us from entering into worship of the Lord. Many people who worship regularly never hear from the Lord, because these spirits have been allowed to take up residence in the building, and in people who are not subject to the Lord Jesus.

DELAYS

On another occasion I decided not to go on that particular Sunday. As the day progressed I felt increasingly that the Lord wanted me to go to the service that evening. About four fifteen that afternoon I decided I would attend the service. The previous Monday I had been studying the word as part of my daily devotions, when out of the scriptures appeared a complete gospel sermon. Occasionally this would happen to me, it usually meant that I was going to receive a telephone call asking me to take a meeting or preach somewhere, so I did what I usually did on these occasions and sought the Lord. However, on this occasion there was no telephone call so I just filed the sermon away and forgot about it until that Sunday evening. What a surprise I had when the Pastor announced the same chapter from the book of Genesis, and then proceeded to preach exactly the same sermon the Lord had given me the previous Monday. After the service I asked the Pastor when the Lord had given him that sermon? His reply surprised me, "four fifteen this afternoon" he said, and then went on to explain he had not been able to find anything to preach about ,until the Lord finally gave him that sermon. That was exactly the time that I had agreed to go to the fellowship that night. I shared with the pastor how the Lord had given me the same word. He was encouraged, but he did say he would prefer to have more notice of what he was to preach on in future!

LESSONS

Through this period in my life I learned several lessons that have stood me in good stead in more recent years. One is, that when we move on, rather than standing still we can make mistakes and travel down wrong roads, or so it seems. However, if we are walking with the Lord we can't really go the wrong way unless like Jonah we get into sin and disobedience.

JONAH

Jonah was told by the Lord to go to Nineveh. Jonah didn't want to go to Nineveh, he knew the Lord wanted to bless the people there. Jonah had other ideas, he decided to go to Tarshish instead. So he set sail only to find the Lord was not pleased with this obvious rebellion. God sent a storm, Jonah knew it was on his account that everyone on board ship was suffering because of his disobedience. Jonah chapter 1 v 8 finds the crew of the ship asking a few questions of Jonah; tell us, who is responsible for making all this trouble for us? What do you do? Where do you come from? What is your country? From what people are you? Jonah shared some testimony with them. He told them he was a Hebrew and worshipped the God of heaven, who made the earth and the sea. They were terrified. The sea was getting rougher and rougher. The crew cried out; What should we do to you, to make the sea calm down. Pick me up, was Jonah's reply and throw me into the sea. When they did the sea went calm. What can we learn from this incident? That even in times of rebellion the Lord can use us. Later on in this chapter from the book of Jonah, we see in vs 14-16 that they cried to the Lord; O Lord, please do not let us die for taking this man's life. Do not hold us accountable for killing an innocent man for you, O. Lord, have done as you pleased. So as we saw they threw Jonah into the sea as V16 tells us. At this the men greatly feared the Lord, and they offered a sacrifice to the Lord and made vows to Him.

A BIG FISH

The Lord saved Jonah too. He provided a big fish to catch and swallow Jonah. Jonah was in the belly of the fish three days and three nights, where eventually he called out to the Lord. In chapter two of Jonah we are told that Jonah repented of his sin,

When we have wilfully gone astray, we too can call out to the Lord as Jonah did. Jonah recognised that his sin had cut him of from God. In chapter 2 v 4 Jonah is recorded as saying; I have been banished from your sight, yet I will look again toward your holy temple. The engulfing waters threatened me, the deep surrounded me, seaweed was wrapped around my head, to the roots of the mountain I sank down, the earth beneath barred me in forever. But you brought me my life up from the pit, O Lord my God. V7 When my life was ebbing away, I remembered you, Lord, and my prayer rose to you, to your holy temple. V9; But I with a song of thanksgiving will sacrifice to you. What I vowed I will make good. Salvation comes from the Lord. When he repented the Lord commanded the fish to spit him out.

SECOND CHANCES

The Lord always gives us a second chance. He gave Jonah another chance, and this time Jonah obeyed and went to Nineveh. When the message of the Lord was proclaimed, the people of Nineveh repented.

Through looking at the life of Jonah, we can see that even if we get it wrong, through wilful disobedience, or by going before the Lord or even just plain misunderstanding what it was the Lord required of us. He does understand and forgives. If he can forgive Jonah's wilful disobedience, His mercy will certainly be extended to us when we get things wrong and take a wrong turning. We can see that the Lord is able to take any situation and use it to His glory. It is better to move on, than to stand still. Standing still can be the result of fear, we become panic stricken, petrified lest we should take the wrong road or maybe like Lot's wife we look back uncertain that we want to go forward. The result if we stay in that place, is that we can turn to a pillar of salt as Lots wife did, or stuck in the mud of fear that grips us. It is better to say "Lord I believe this is the way to go, if I have got it wrong, will you turn me around" The Lord knows our heart. If we are honest before Him, He will continue to lead and guide us, using even the detours we make to His glory.

Going back to the village I had lived in as a child, and being willing to live there, showed me how much the Lord had healed me and set me free from many fears and bad memories. Memories of fears, developed as I walked the mile and a half from the school bus each day, to our home in the country. My childish imagination had worked overtime as I walked alone down dark country roads with no street lights, I would imagine a ghost behind every tree and bush, waiting to jump out and attack me! Fear of being attacked overwhelmed me as I ran home on dark winter nights, passed the darkened shape of trees and bushes.

FORGIVENESS

The Lord overcame the shame I felt in going back. While we were living outside this village, my life had been one of taunting, ridicule and rejection. By the grace of God it has not hindered me from accomplishing what He had planned and purposed for me. I remembered my own shame as I returned to that village where the shame of being caught stealing sweets from the local shop had taken place. All these memories and many more came flooding back, to haunt me once again. However, through that detour came healing and forgiveness. Forgiveness for my sins, forgiveness toward my parents, my school tormentors, the teachers who did nothing to protect me from the bullies, and finally I forgave myself. I was free from this part of the past I had faced up to it with Jesus holding my hand. I could let it all go. Detours can be good for you, when they are a gift from God. If you find you have gone the wrong way, check, did you wilfully go that way, or was it the Lord's providence to enable Him and you, to deal with areas in your life that He could get at in no other way.

Similarly, in my excursions to the fellowship I had attended on Sunday evenings during this period of my life it had appeared to have been a wrong turning. In fact it was part of His blessing for that fellowship who, as a result of my binding those evil spirits and loosing the Holy Spirit into their midst, came into a new walk with the Lord.

CHAPTER 12

One day I was looking in the local newspaper in the houses for sale column. When there it was! The house I had seen in my vision— well nearly! The house was the same style, it had five bedrooms, but the drive was on the right of the house and not the left. I made an appointment to see the house the next day. With great excitement I drove to the avenue where the house was located. It was so exciting to see at last, the house I had held in my mind for so many years.

THE BATHROOM

Going into the house was equally as exciting for the interior was even more wonderful than I had expected. We walked through the house, the owner, estate agent, Jim and myself. There was a bedroom down stairs just as I had visualised, a bathroom, a laundry and beautiful kitchen, in addition to a very large lounge/ dining room. Upstairs were four more bedrooms including one with its own bathroom, in addition to a separate bathroom. In the vision I had seen several rooms in the house and was very clear as to the colour of one bathroom. However, I had no knowledge of what the lounge or kitchen were like. I had an impression of the garden to the rear of the house, being special, but I had no visualisation of it. This garden however was small, and by no means special. Later I visited the house again for a second time . Because of my lack of knowledge of how accurate the actual premises should be to the original visualisation. I decided to telephone Gary Stevenson, the Pastor who had previously been so helpful in the earlier years with encouraging me to press on with prayer to break through point.

Again Gary was very helpful. This is what he told me. Firstly the exterior of the house in the vision, was likely to be of a style I particularly like, though the house the Lord had for me was likely to look different externally than I had visualised

COMPLICATIONS

When it comes to premises , a house for example, it is possible in a vision to see the property as it was on that day I had the vision in 1984, to see it as it would be when we moved in to the property in 1999. The house could also contain features and improvements we might make in the future. So in effect expect to see a different exterior, but the rooms would be of the number I had seen, and one bathroom that I had gone into was likely to be as I had seen it in the vision. So this could be the house.

Jim and I talked it over and I prayed that we might know what the house was to be used for. The Lord had told me that all the furniture and furnishings had to be new. Would the house be used in a caring capacity, as a house for the elderly or maybe for those with severe learning disabilities both of whom I had with worked with in the past. Maybe the Lord wanted it used for something else, all we knew was the occupants would initially be strangers to us. How would we know if this was the right house?

TEMPERAMENT

Perhaps more importantly was Jim of the right temperament to be involved in a project like this. During the two years we had been married, he had shown an instability that was frightening to say the least, and he was becoming increasingly violent. As I prayed I knew I could not subject anyone else, to this type of behaviour, particularly those who needed caring for. Reluctantly and sadly I came to the conclusion that I would have to lay down the vision, so I gave it back to the Lord. In doing so I expected that I would not now come into the vision. I had married Jim believing it was the Lord's will for us, and it was a marriage I intended to see through, until death parted us. I didn't say anything of my decision to Jim, neither wanting to upset him or hurt him.

The next day I returned home from work, Jim wasn't home, he was a shift worker , and was on late shift that day, he would be back from work about ten thirty that night.

KEYS

My daughter and her baby son came to tea that day. The baby was crawling around the floor, into everything as usual, when we heard him playing with some keys behind the front door, which led into the lounge.

At first I thought they were my daughter's keys, when she looked at them she realised they were not hers, then she recognised them as Jim's keys. I couldn't understand why Jim's keys should be behind the door. I went upstairs to the bedroom , Jim's pyjamas were on the bed, every thing seemed as normal. But he didn't come home that night.

CHAPTER 13

When Jim didn't return I wasn't unduly worried, he had often got up out of bed in the middle of the night and disappeared without any explanation. He would return after completing which ever shift he had been on; he would return as though he had just left that morning. If I attempted to ask where he had gone, I was told to mind my own business, or just ignored. So I learned to live peaceably with the situation.

MISSING

Several days later a friend came to tea, and I confided in her of Jim's disappearance. Had I phoned his work she asked. No, I hadn't. I didn't want the embarrassment of it or, if Jim heard about it, the violence that would follow. Still she insisted I should do something. So I telephoned his place of work, only to be told that he hadn't been in work that week and they hadn't heard from him either.

At that point I telephoned the police and told them the story. They said they would come round to the house, but first, would I check if his driving licence, passport and bank book were there in the house before they came round. I hadn't previously looked among Jim's personal effects because he did not like me to go into what he considered to be his belongings, so I had learned to stay away from his possessions. But now I had to look because the police needed to know what he had taken with him. His possessions were laid out very tidily in the drawer with space between each item, as I looked

I realised his bank book , driving licence and passport were missing. I noticed the box that the wedding ring I had bought him was at the back of the drawer. I don't know why I opened the box, because the ring was on his finger when I left for work the morning that he disappeared, but there in the box was the wedding ring.

The police arrived and asked a few questions, and I told them about the missing documents, the keys behind the door and the wedding ring. The policemen said; "we are sorry to tell you that he has planned all this and he has gone; he has left you." Two weeks went by and still I had heard nothing. He hadn't returned to work, nobody had seen or heard from him, so I sent for the police again.

Two different policemen came. I told them the story and their response was the same as the first two policemen, "but how can you say that" I asked, "he's left all his clothes behind, his pyjamas were still on the bed, his toothbrush and shaving things still in the bathroom". But they assured me that while it looked like he had killed himself, they didn't believe so, in fact they believed he had deliberately planned this and made it look like he had killed himself and that's what he wanted me to believe.

IS THIS LOVE

I couldn't understand this. How could someone say they love you, and yet put you through this sort of torment?

One day I decided to visit our doctor. He had spent some time with Jim the previous year. At that time I had been concerned by Jim's behaviour and had wondered if there was some physical problem which accounted for his behaviour. The doctor decided that the only way to get Jim to the doctor's surgery was to ask him to attend to have a check done on his cholesterol levels. There was a national campaign on at the time, so Jim had no suspicions of what the doctor was really trying to discover. Jim went along to the doctors. When he didn't return for nearly two hours, I thought maybe he had gone somewhere else after the doctors. When I visited the doctors after Jim's disappearance, I asked the doctor if Jim was likely to kill himself? I hadn't told the doctor of Jim's disappearance. His reply was rather startling, "No", he had said he wouldn't kill himself, but I'll tell you what he will do, he will disappear. Surprised, I told him that's exactly what he had done, and I went on to explain the situation. "I've been expecting that to happen". Now, I'll tell you something; you are a very lucky lady, because my practice nurse and myself spent an hour and a half with Jim the day he came to the surgery, and our belief was that he intended to kill you. You must be very careful, because he may still try!" The Lord had protected me so often, over the past two years, of that I had been aware.

STAY STILL—DON'T MOVE

There had been times when I knew that if I had not obeyed the Holy Spirit's prompting, I would not be writing this now. In my spirit I knew what the doctor was saying was true , so many times the Holy Spirit had prompted me to say nothing , "stay still, or don't move". Thankfully, I had not been aware of Jim's real intention toward me, but had obeyed the Holy Spirit and so had been kept safe. At times I had been fearful, but not as fearful as I would have been if I had known Jim's real intention towards me.

We are often not aware of why the Holy Spirit prompts us , but we can be sure that it is only for our good .Recently a friend shared with us that on one occasion he was driving down a certain road, when the Holy Spirit clearly said to him, turn right at the next junction, but he was attracted by some event that he knew was taking place further down the road he was travelling along, He decided he wanted to see what was going on. It was something he had been involved in before he came to know the Lord, and he was tempted to see if things had changed at all in the scene from his past. Then it happened, Bang! a car came from nowhere, straight into his car. Now he knew why the Holy Spirit had wanted him to go down the other road — it was safer. Listening to the promptings of the Holy Spirit are vital to all of us, for not only does he lead us into all truth, but He also guards us along the way. Who knows how many accidents or unfortunate happenings we would have been involved in, but for the gracious protection of our Lord.?

THE WILDERNESS IS OVER

Earlier that year Bob Gordon a well known Christian speaker and author had visited our fellowship to take a weekend of meetings for church leaders. I had often been blessed by his writings , but I hardly saw myself as a church leader, but I asked the Pastor if I could attend the meetings. His response was encouraging. Yes, he expected me to be there as he saw me as a church leader. What a joy to be in the meeting. The worship that night was quite special, lifting us into the Lord's presence. When Bob Gordon began to speak, he started by saying that the Lord had told him not to say what he had planned to say, but that the Lord had a message for this group. He started by saying, several of you here think you have lost your way in your walk with the Lord, but you haven't. You have forgotten that the Lord sent you into the wilderness and you're not lost. You are going through a time of preparation and will soon come out of the wilderness experience. Wow! The Lord had spoken not just to me, but to several others who I knew were going through their own times of testing, and the Lord had said it was nearly over.

When Jim left me this was the end of my testing. Once again I had no husband, no money, and I was left to pay the bills— where was he?

A VISITOR

In late May I went to visit a friend who lived in a nearby town. It was her birthday, and I went to take her some flowers. We had a lovely afternoon together. When I arrived home that evening I made myself a sandwich and a drink , and ate it watching television. A little later I took my plate and cup through to the kitchen to wash them and as I walked across the kitchen floor towards the sink, I noticed an empty milk bottle by the side of the sink. So what's so unusual about that you may ask? Well nothing except I never drink milk and if I am having visitors who do, I buy a carton of milk from the supermarket. I never buy milk in a bottle, so how did the bottle get there? Perhaps one of the children had made a visit while I was out. The two who lived locally both had keys to the house. So I thought no more about it.

Jim had now been missing ten weeks, with no word to anyone of his whereabouts, except what the police had been able to pick up on their checks through bank records.

ANOTHER VISIT

Two weeks later, after visiting friends, I returned home in the early evening. The first thing I noticed when I walked into the kitchen was that where there had been one empty milk bottle placed by the sink, there were now two empty milk bottles, Why, how? I phoned my daughter to see if she had been to visit while I had been out. No, she hadn't been down today. I then telephoned my eldest son and asked him the same question, then I told him about the milk bottles, "Mum" he said "you know what this means?" I was beginning to. Jim must have had another set of keys cut before he left and was coming into the house while I was out. "Go" my son said "to the local DIY store, it will still be open, and get a new lock. I'm coming over to change the lock." Just in time the lock was changed. The following Sunday while I was at church, Jim tried to get into the house. For the first time in three months, Jim was sighted, not once but three times in three different locations on the same day. It was obvious from the sightings that he had been to the house and then made his way back to his mother's house.

Two days later he telephoned to say he was at his mothers house. It was his birthday!

When I told the Pastor that Jim had reappeared, he said he believed the Lord would have me divorce him; "do it now" he said, "while you know where he is and can serve the divorce papers on him", so I did.

I HATE DIVORCE

Now this was my second divorce as a Christian and I was devastated. I remember one day while I was out walking, looking down at my body and seeing this enormous hole. It was as though an Exocet missile had gone straight through me. I remember thinking how clean cut the hole was! God says in the book of Malachi chapter two v 16; I hate divorce. I too can say with all my heart, I hate divorce. It is one of the most destructive things anyone can go through. God hates divorce but loves those who are divorced. He also has a plan to move you on from where you are now into the purposes He has for you. He knows you are hurting. He knows the pain you feel. He knows the rejection of divorce. He knows because He has been there. The book of Hosea is the story of the divorce between God and His people. It tells us of His pain. His despair. But it also tells us of His on going love for His bride. The Jews are still part of the bride of Christ. The Lord is wooing them back to Himself. He still has a plan and purpose for their life. They are still the apple of His eye. When God speaks of divorce in the book of Malachi, he speaks of His hatred of divorce. Divorce is not only between man and woman. When we fail to be totally committed to the Lord and when we only allow Him into certain areas of our lives, we are in effect divorcing Him from our lives. We say to the Lord "You can come to church with me, however, I don't want you involved in my work life or my business deals." This lack of commitment is a divorce from the Lord. We need to allow Him into every area of our life, have total integrityand be being fully integrated. Wholly one with Him.

Just as a marriage covenant between a man and a woman should be kept faithfully, so our marriage covenant with the bridegroom, the Lord Jesus Christ, should be one of faithfulness and total commitment.

SEVENTY TIMES SEVEN

The amazing thing about this chapter in my life, is that I came out of it a better person. Mark who is the son of some close friends of mine, was seven at the time he prophesied that marrying Jim would be the making of me! Out of the mouths of babes, we often say. On this occasion there was more than a grain of truth in it. The Lord used all that I went through to His greater glory. Through it, He taught me many lessons. Peter asked Jesus; How many times must we forgive, seven times? Jesus said , no, seventy times seven, that is about every two minutes of our working day. Think of it, every time someone stands on your toes or offends you in any way, no matter how often, we have to forgive. The sixth chapter of Matthew's gospel contains some interesting and challenging words. These words are well known to us all we recite them frequently when we say the Lord's prayer, but have we really understood them? V12; Forgive us our debts, as we have forgiven our debtors. These words from the prayer Jesus taught His disciples are very clear. First we have to forgive those who sin against us before we can be forgiven. Many people today, sadly do not walk with the Lord in this light. How often do we hear the hardness of heart that states "I'll never forgive that person." We hold grudges against a brother or sister and believe it is our right to do so. The penalty for not forgiving is clear. If we don't forgive others, neither will our Father in heaven forgive us. The Lord through the Holy Spirit taught me early on in my Christian walk to keep short accounts with those who offended in any way, "keep forgiving" he would say. I don't pretend that this is always easy. Some things that happen in our lives are so hurtful that it seems that we will never be able to forgive. However, by the grace of the Lord and the enabling of the Holy Spirit we can forgive. The same power that enabled Jesus to say. Father forgive them for they know not what they do. He said this as He hung crucified on the cross. This power is available to us. It takes an act of will to forgive, but we must will to do so.

GRACE

When this period of my life had drawn to a close, my Pastor commented on the fact that I didn't seem bitter about what had happened, and I wasn't. The grace of God is sufficient for all our needs, and once again His grace proved to be all I needed. I was able to forgive and keep forgiving, even during the worst moments. Another lesson I learned was to listen to and obey the Holy Spirit. In my case it meant the difference between life and death. To hear and obey was to live, to not have heard or disobeyed would have been certain death.

CHAPTER 14

It was September 1993 when the Lord challenged me again. He said "If you don't give up work, you won't come into my plans and purposes."

This was six months after Jim had left. I had a mortgage to pay, a car on hire purchase and the usual living expenses. I had been in my job for more than two years, I had a good salary with a pension. I was working for the local Training and Enterprise council, as a business adviser. I had an office on the outskirts of Manchester, with a team of advisers and administrative staff.

GIVE UP WORK

During the previous nine months, I had become increasingly tired and lethargic. I put it down to having had a double dose of flu the previous winter. In addition to all the other difficulties in my life I thought I just needed a holiday, so I went with my daughter, her husband and their little boy to Tenerife thinking this would revive me. However, the reverse happened. Once I had stopped work, I couldn't get going again, and I had to have a month on sick leave. Returning to work a month later wasn't easy. I became increasingly tired and drained. When the Lord spoke to me about giving up work, I had no hesitation in agreeing, but I did say to the Lord, "Lord you will have to work it out, because as you know I have no savings or income other than my salary." Within three days, four different people asked me if I thought I had M.E. or chronic fatigue syndrome.

Well, I didn't know what M.E. was, let alone if that was what I was suffering from. I visited the doctor and asked him that question. He suggested that I visit a consultant who specialised in these illnesses. At the same time the company I worked for decided to send me to another consultant. Within ten days I saw two consultants, who both said I had M.E. Both recommended I gave up working. Which I did immediately. The Lord had done it. When I had asked him to sort it out I didn't expect to lose my job quite so quickly. Now I just had to wait upon the Lord and see what he would do next.

LIVING WITH M.E.

During late October it seemed like my brain closed down. I couldn't do anything, I was so exhausted all the time. Then I couldn't think or remember anything. Thankfully on the Sunday before Christmas, I woke up and realised my brain was functioning properly again.

The problem now was I still couldn't remember things very well. How did my computer switch on, how did I get into a programme I needed? I couldn't remember, how to operate the printer. My daughter had to write everything down for me. Little by little my memory began to return.

The new year was going to be special as I had planned to go to Israel with a group from the fellowship I belonged to. Now the problem was would I be able to cope with the travelling? Trips to Israel I knew could be tiring.

THE LORD PROVIDES

An even greater problem was where was the money going to come from? I didn't have any, and I needed more than seven hundred pounds for the holiday. I believed the Lord was going to provide. Now it was February we were due to leave for Israel the next month. My Pastor reassured me that the Lord was going to provide.

As I sought the Lord for the finance, I felt he was saying to look at the small print of the bank loan I had taken out to buy my car. For several days I didn't bother checking because I had never take out insurance to cover sickness, etc., when I had previously had a bank loan. However, the voice persisted; look at the policy it said. When I did, I was surprised to discover that the payments were covered by an insurance that would cover the payments while I was sick. How wonderful that the Lord knows everything. The sickness cover payment was back dated to the time I first became ill. So this was how I got my money to pay for my first visit to Israel

The next concern was would my health stand up to a gruelling tour of Israel, with much climbing of hills and walking. Not only did the Lord enable me but strengthened me sufficiently to be able to walk down from the top of Masada, which though down hill was no easy walk, but nonetheless a great blessing. Visiting Israel for the first time was wonderful. To see the land of the Bible was a thrilling experience

ISRAEL

On the first day in Israel we went to the area where David had killed Goliath. The coach drew up at the side of the road in the valley of Elan, the guide pointed to a brook and said; "Over there is the brook that David probably took the stones to kill Goliath". My friend, who was sat next to me, suddenly sat up in her seat and said 'you mean it really happened?' She was amazed she thought Bible stories where myths. Alma had been brought up in the Catholic Church and had attended a Catholic school , were she had been taught Bible stories were myths. Three years before our visit to Israel, Alma had come to know Jesus as her Saviour. There in the Elan valley the scales of deception that had been there for nearly fifty years fell from her eyes. The Lord touched her spirit so mightily that day, that she just hungered for the truth of the word. During the week Alma learned more and more about the Bible and the activities of the people recorded there. During the weeks itinerary a visit was planned to Yardinet, one of the baptismal sites on the river Jordan.

Helen Rylance

BAPTISM

Alma started to question me about why baptism was carried out. I was able to share with her, that it is a sign to the world that we have been buried with Christ, and raised to newness of life. Did she need to be baptised she wanted to know; after all she was baptised as a baby. I told her that this was something her parents had done to bring her to God. Now as an adult she was responsible for deciding if she would be obedient to the word of the Lord. We looked at the sermon of Peter recorded in the book of the Acts of the Apostles chapter two v 38) where Peter had replied; Repent and be baptised, every one of you, in the name of Jesus Christ for the forgiveness of sins. And you will receive the gift of the Holy Spirit. She knew she had repented, and her sins had been forgiven but she had not been baptised. She decided to ask the Pastor of our group if he was willing to baptise her in the River Jordan, and he agreed. We hadn't been aware that people had been listening as I shared the scriptures with Alma. A lady from Wales had overheard our conversations, regarding baptism. She told us she had wanted to be baptised for many years, believing that this is what the Lord required of her. She had wanted to be obedient, but because she belonged to a denomination that did not encourage believers to be baptised, the opportunity had not arisen. Now here was the answer to her desire to be obedient. The Pastor listened to the testimonies of faith given by both ladies. He could not doubt their sincerity, and agreed to baptise them both on the following Saturday in the River Jordan. In my heart I longed to be able to take part in Alma's baptism, but felt because I was a woman I probably wouldn't be asked. However, I prayed thinking that maybe the Lord would speak to the Pastor. How delighted I was next day when the Pastor asked me to assist him in baptising the two ladies. Yes, this indeed was turning out to be a trip of a lifetime or was it?

CHAPTER 15

Later that year Israel beckoned again. Life had been difficult since my return from Israel in March my illness had continued to take its course. By this time I had lost my job because of my inability to function effectively. The doctor's diagnosis was that I would never work again. The question was, would my condition worsen? Would I end up in a wheel chair as had been predicted? These were questions I often asked. However, the Lord had said that if I gave up my job I would come into his plans and purposes. I reminded myself of this frequently.

SEEK FIRST HIS KINGDOM

One day a word of scripture came alive to me as I was reading Matthew chapter six, when those well known words really struck me. Verse 33 says; But seek first His kingdom and His righteousness, and all these things will be given to you as well. Prior to this verse Jesus was saying to His disciples, look I know that you need food and clothing. Look around you, look at the birds, the flowers, I know what they need. How much more then do I know your needs, look to Me first, seek the things of My kingdom, seek My ways of doing things, then I will give you all that you have need of. Suddenly, it was as if Jesus had said, come to Me, seek Me, when you find Me, then all that you have need of will be given you.

When I began to seek Him with all my heart, things began to change, I wasn't sleeping quite as long, I was able to think more clearly and had a little more energy. At least now I could wash—up after each meal, instead of leaving them until I had the energy to deal with them. I was able to make an occasional meal, instead of taking a frozen meal from the freezer and heating it in the microwave, as I had been doing for the past year.

Then my younger son Andrew told me he was going to Israel in January. We talked about where he was staying and the sites he would be visiting. I began to feel the pull to go back to Israel again as the Lord called me. However, where would I get the money from? And would my son want his mother tagging along? After all he was a grown man.

OFF TO ISRAEL AGAIN

Yes, the Lord did want me to go to Israel. Then came what was to become the perennial question; where am I going to get the money from Lord? This time he pointed me to an insurance policy that was due for paying out, so my financial needs were met. Andrew said "It's OK I don't mind." Later he was to say to me, "I'm really glad you came, you were the sanest person in the group." Quite a compliment when you consider, he like the rest of the group were clergymen and their wives or husbands. This time we were to stay in Tiberias and Jerusalem. On my first visit we had stayed at the seaside town of Netanya and travelled to the various Biblical and historic sites. We covered a lot of the country, but each day lasted up to twelve hours, which made it a long tiring day. On this trip because the travelling would be less, it wouldn't be quite as tiring. However, it was a training course for those who wanted to become group leaders taking groups of pilgrims on tours of Israel.

Our guide on the first trip had been quite knowledgeable about the history of the land, but as a non religious Jew she did not have a great deal of Biblical knowledge, but the information she shared with us was a good basis for the second trip. Moshe was our guide, an eminent archaeologist, who had spent many years sifting through various ancient ruins in Israel this combined with his knowledge of the Bible, left you hungering for more information, and increased our love of the land. We hung on to his every word, his knowledge of the land of Israel and the Bible was awesome; he really brought the Bible alive for us.

JESUS—A JEW

When I had visited Israel the previous year, two things had struck me. I often share with people these two things because they are so obvious and yet for me at that time such an awesome revelation, that the marvel of it has never left me. The first was Jesus was a Jew. "So what, you may say." I had never thought of Him as having dark hair and eyes, and wearing the clothing of a rabbi of His day. For me Jesus was as He is portrayed in much western art, as blond haired with blue eyes, just as we have so often seen Him portrayed in films. The second discovery was to be more profound.

THE PRISONER

On a visit to St Peter Gallacantu in Jerusalem. We visited a church built on the remains of what was believed to be Caiphas the high priest's house. It is believed that it was in the court yard of this house that Peter denied that he knew Jesus. We arrived to find the site being excavated. The site was thought to be the high priest's house at the time of Jesus crucifixion. A doorway had been made in an external lower wall. We were allowed to go inside. What I saw that day changed my whole view of the Bible. The room we went into was about four metres high, not a large room. However, there were no doors or windows the only entrance point into this room was through a hole in the ceiling. We were told this was probably where Jesus spent His last night on earth. I was shocked. Jesus had spent His last night here, but this was a dungeon it had no doors or windows. Were there beds in here? No, Jesus spent the night on the floor, with the other prisoners, like a common criminal, At the best He had been let down on a rope through the hole in the ceiling at worst He was pushed through the hole to fall on the hard ground below. Then the next day brought up on a rope, back through the hole to face the last day of His life on earth, and all the horror that entailed. I couldn't wait to get back to my hotel room to check what it said in the Bible about Jesus stay at Caiphas's house.

I couldn't believe what I read in John chapter nineteen v 28; Then they led Jesus from the house of Caiaphas to the praetorian. It was early. That was all, nothing there to give a clue as to what I had just seen. A dark, dirty room, no doors, no doubt infested with rats and cockroaches and fleas for company, to say nothing of His fellow prisoners, violent men, thugs and drunks. What happened that night? Did Jesus tell them of the Kingdom of God? I'm sure He did. How must he have felt having shed blood of such quantity that it fell to the ground in great drops, having experienced the betrayal of one of His disciples, Judas. Also one of His closest friends and disciples Peter, who three times denied he knew Him, just as Jesus had predicted he would. Down in that pit, did He think about the decision He had made earlier that evening to carry the sins of the world, your sins and mine, so that we might be reconciled to the Father and have a relationship with Him and the Father. Did He realise that this was but the beginning of what He was to suffer for our sakes? Knowing how indifferent we were to become to His sufferings. I count it a privilege that I was able to see that room before it became glamorised as it is today. I never forgot that experience because it made me realise that the Bible is the most understated book ever written. It gave me a zest to know more about the land and the people. Most of all it gave me a desire to know Jesus better. To understand what He meant by His words, what was behind them, how they apply today. My search to know Jesus better had begun. I began to seek Him first, then His kingdom, followed by His righteousness. After spending another week in Israel in the presence of a guide who knew the Bible, the land and the people began to take on a new meaning. Now I wanted to share Israel with everybody. My desire was to take a group of people to the land, to lead them into a deeper understanding of the word of God, His people, the Jews and the land.

ANOTHER VISIT

In the following February, a group of fifteen of us left England for Israel on a cold winter's day. I had been asked to take Barbara with me. Barbara was in her fifties and had Downs syndrome. She longed to go to Israel, but because of her learning disability she wasn't able to go on her own as she needed assistance to get through the practicalities of life. Her Mother was in her eighties and felt she couldn't make the trip so she asked if I would take her. What could I say?

When we left Manchester for Israel that Monday, I had no idea what the Lord had in store for us. Barbara had two ambitions; one was to ride a camel, the other to float in the Dead sea. Both these she achieved during the week. However, the Lord had planned other surprises for her. Were these the secret desires of her heart?

JESUS COMES

We had been on the aeroplane less than an hour when Barbara started to talk about God. One thing led to another, as I found myself sharing the gospel with her. Despite her lack of education and limited communication skills, she was able to grasp what I was saying. She had been a member of the Church of England most of her adult life, she frequently attended church. But she didn't know Jesus personally. As I talked about Him it was obvious she understood the way of the cross and the need for salvation. At the end of our conversation, she simply said, "Will Jesus come into my life if I ask Him to?" When I led her in the sinner's prayer, she said, "Oh! He's come I can feel the Holy Spirit." What joy as she accepted Jesus as her Saviour. The power of the Holy Spirit filled her and gave her His peace. During the week, mainly in the night the Lord revealed Himself to her as the Lamb of God, Jesus appeared to her in person, she was able to describe this person. She saw an angel and finally the rider on a white horse. Were these genuine sightings? I believe so. Barbara didn't have the Biblical knowledge to invent such visions. In the night in a room on her own, she was quite fearful. I believe the Lord comforted her with His presence appearing to her in these various forms that those of us who can read would recognise from the Bible. Barbara however, had no such knowledge. How loving our Lord is to bring us the comfort we need, when we need it.

MARY

Mary was in her eighties when she went to Israel with our little group. One evening after dinner several of us were sat around singing choruses'. Various ones would lead in a hymn or chorus as it came to mind. Mary started to sing a golden oldie one of the lines of the song said," I m S.A.V.E.D. I 'm S.A.V.E.D. I know I am I'M sure I am I 'm S.A.V.E.D." Mary hadn't been coming to our fellowship long and I knew very little about her. I had never heard her testify to Jesus being in her life, but as she led us in this little song, I felt to ask her quietly and privately if she knew Jesus as her Saviour. A little later I was able to ask her, if the song had real meaning for her. She told me that when she was seven years of age, seventy five years previously she had asked Jesus to forgive her sins and come into her life. When I asked her if she had ever shared this with anyone. She said no I was the first. I shared a verse with her from the book of Romans chapter ten v10; For it is with your heart that you believe and are justified, and it is with your mouth that you confess and are saved. Jesus said if you confess me before men I will confess you before the Father. In seventy five years Mary had never told anyone, not even her son who is a Christian and a church elder, that she had asked Jesus into her life. Consequently, Jesus had not been able to own her as his own until that day in Israel. How we rejoiced over this lost sheep. Mary came into a new joy, knowing she was beloved of the Lord, accepted at last, known by the Father and Son, acknowledged as a child of God .

The vision kept coming back to me. The Lord kept reminding

me that despite the apparent reversals of my life the vision was still to be fulfilled. One day a friend telephoned me to ask if I had seen an advertisement in a Christian magazine, I hadn't so she gave me the information. Christian Guest house for sale or rent ran the advertisement, and gave a box number for further information. The house was situated in a small village on the North west coast of England, about one hundred and twenty miles from where I lived. I wrote to the box number given in the advertisement, and waited. The next week I received a reply to my letter. The letter contained details of the property and an invitation to visit the property. Keith and Diana the owners sent me directions to the house and a date was set for my visit.

A CHALLENGE

The village was a lovely coastal resort, with few tourists around. Nor many ventured from the nearby Lake District. Keith and Diana and I shared our respective stories over a cup of coffee and I met the visitors to the guest house, most of whom were there long term. We looked around the house. It was three storeys high, a terraced house with a back yard. Everything was of good taste and quality, but was this what the Lord wanted for me? At this point of time I was still sleeping twelve hours a night and part of the day too. Would I be able to look after this place keeping it clean, cooking and washing as well. I didn't really feel the guest house was meant for me. However, when I heard Keith and Diana story I felt led to offer my services as a relief worker to give them a much needed break. They had no one to take over from them, and had been on duty for several months without a break. So we agreed that I would visit the guest house the following weekend to learn how to run the place.

LIGHT

What had I been thinking of when I offered to help out? Here I was vacuuming the stairs, red in the face from exertion. It was a particularly difficult house to clean. I realised how unfit I really had become over the last two and a half years, having done very little of my own housework. Why did I think I could tackle someone else's? Ironing the clothes was an additional problem. My illness had affected my muscles and bones. Which meant using my arms for any physical activity resulted in long nights of agony, as agonising pains ran through my muscles and bones. I wanted to get fit and well again to come into God's plans for me, so I persisted. When I had completed my trial run of looking after the house with Keith and Diana in attendance, we decided that I could probably manage on my own. So we arranged that the following weekend they would go away and leave me to hold the fort. By the grace of God and his enabling and strength, I was able to take over the running of the house on a regular basis for many months. Eventually I became fitter, even though I was still sleeping twelve hours a night, I was beginning to feel there was light at the end of the tunnel.

CHAPTER 16

During July 1996 there was a great deal on the television news about a battle going on in Drumcree, Northern Ireland. While watching the news bulletins I could sense the Holy Spirit moving in me and praying through me. Every day for a week this carried on. I would watch the news reports on the television. Each time the Holy Spirit would move on me stirring me up, but without any verbal prayer but praying through my Spirit. On the Saturday as I was watching the news again, the Holy Spirit spoke to me "Write it down" he said. "Write what down?" I asked. "Just get a pen and paper and write down what I tell you." So I got a pen and paper and began to write whatever came to me. When I looked at what I had written I realised it was a call to repentance for the British nation from its sin toward Northern Ireland and its people. "Lord," I prayed "what do you want me to do with this," The Lord responded by telling me to "Take it to small interdenominational prayer groups up and down the land, starting in your home town." There was just one problem. I didn't know where there was one in my home town, let alone throughout the country.

WHERE TO START?

Where to start, what to do next I didn't know so I prayed. I felt I should go and talk to my Pastor which is always a good starting point. So I sought out my Pastor and shared with him what the Lord had given me. His first question was "what do you know about Irish history?" "Nothing" was my reply I had always hated history when

I was at school. "Well I suggest you start reading up on the history of Ireland, you can hardly go around calling on people to repent , when you know nothing about what they are to repent of. Then he said he would give me a letter giving his approval for me to do this work. I was to send a copy of the "Call to repentance" and his letter to everyone I could think of. Meanwhile, I was to ask Gary and Dilys Stevenson what they thought of it. (I have mentioned Gary elsewhere in the book). He and his wife are Irish, one from the south of Ireland and one from the north of Ireland. This is the message I sent to them;

THE MESSAGE

We are to repent.

The whole of the United Kingdom and those in Southern Ireland, of the following, We in England, Scotland and Wales are to repent of our attitude to the Irish people as a whole.

We are to repent of the sins of our forefathers, as we and they have cursed the whole of Ireland and its people through our actions in the past.

The people of both North and South Ireland are to repent of their attitude toward each other.

Catholic and Protestants who love the Lord Jesus are to repent of their sin toward each other, for example, distrust, suspicion, etc.

The Irish people as a whole are to repent on behalf of their ancestors of the curses placed upon each other in the past, specifically those who love the Lord Jesus, are to repent of their own and their ancestors' involvement in any battle or event in the past that has resulted in marches being carried out today.

We are to repent, forgive each other and be reconciled in Christ Jesus our Lord.

Through public repentance, forgiveness and reconciliation, there will be a public spectacle made of the enemy, in doing so the darkness over the whole of Ireland will be broken and dispersed and the Lord will bless the land.

MY HEART SANK

The reply I received back from the Stephenson's was interesting. They felt that the people of Ireland would not like the part that talked about the need to repent of their sin in marching through each other's territory and causing their enemies upset as a result of this marching. My heart sank, maybe the Lord hadn't really given me the message anyway. As I prayed the Lord told me to turn the book of Obadiah v13; The Amplified Bible states You should not have entered the gates of my people in the day of their calamity and ruin, yes, you should not have looked with delight on their misery in the day of their calamity. The Lord was clearly stating that it was wrong of the Irish people to have these marches, and adopt the attitude that they do as they march. This has for so many years caused so much trouble amongst both Catholic and Protestant communities. While those who hold these marches and organise them would say that they have every right to march through their rival's streets, and that is so. What the Lord said was you should not do this in the manner that you have done for so many years. Both sides of the divide march with the intent of inciting their rivals. This is obvious by the gestures, remarks and disdain that are shown by these groups. The Lord showed me clearly from scripture that what they were doing was wrong, and this should be repented of, and stopped. Interestingly the Stevensons felt that the people would not repent of their actions, and by and large they didn't, with one exception. One man I met at one of the prayer meetings I visited in England felt led to repent of his involvement in the marches. Wherever I took the message people repented of every thing in the message, not by my prompting I might add, because I would just read the word and leave the Holy Spirit to do the rest. Nothing has changed in Northern Ireland, with regard to the marching but it will as various groups lay down their right to march.

MARANATHA

I began to share with people in my fellowship what the Lord was saying regarding repentance and the need to take this message out. Norris, one of our deacons told me of an interdenominational organisation who had a prayer group in the town. It's name was Maranatha, a Manchester based organisation, who met on a regular basis all around Britain. I contacted the local representative and I asked if I could share with their group this message. When she knew of the contents, she became excited as they, as an organisation, had received a similar word from the Lord earlier in the year, asking them to make a call for repentance on this issue of the nation's sin toward Ireland and her people.

A SHOCK TO THE SYSTEM

I was invited to accompany them on a tour of the churches of Northern Ireland, where I would be able to encourage the believers with the message I had been given. What a shock to my system this tour was going to be! As I looked at the itinerary for the next ten days I realised I would need the Lord to uphold me if I was to accomplish this schedule. It was evident from the itinerary that there was little time to stop to eat, let alone sleep. Each day started with morning prayers, team briefings and breakfast, usually by eight am we had packed the cars up with the materials we were taking with us, then we were away on the road, often attending four or five meetings a day, travelling the length and breadth of Northern Ireland. Gone was my twelve hours of sleep; now I was lucky if I got five hours. However, the Lord wonderfully blessed me. As I went out in faith, trusting for my daily portion of health and strength, so it was granted. I never felt overly tired just healthily tired at the end of each day.

This was to be my foretaste of life on the road, travelling from group to group of those who interceded for the people of Northern Ireland. At meetings that I didn't preach or teach, I just read the message the Lord had given, calling those present as the Lord had led. It was amazing to see the Lord lead His people in prayers of repentance often with tears. When I read the message, I did not share the specific things the Lord had told me needed repenting of. One example was telling jokes at the expense of the Irish, too many jokes are told with no thought of whether the Irish may be belittled or defamed by these jokes. One night at a meeting in Leeds, Yorkshire, a lady actually repented of telling Irish jokes. The Holy Spirit had convicted her.

WAR

Many more areas of life were repented of. Those who had been sent to Ireland at the end of the 1914—1918 war, repented on behalf of their ancestors who had been sent to Dublin in the South of Ireland to quell the riots, which ended in shooting indiscriminately, men, women and children. These had been young raw soldiers, sent to the South of Ireland, these soldiers sickened by what they had seen in the war, were sent to calm things down. Children of such men spoke of how their father's lives had been haunted by what they had been commanded to do. Others who had been in the British army in more recent years, repented of their sin toward the Irish. Orange men repented of their sin of their involvement in these organisations. One lady found herself taken back to the years of the potato famine that was responsible for thousands dying of starvation in Ireland in the 1800s. She knew nothing of this part of history, and yet was led by the Holy Spirit to repent of her family's involvement in the corruption of that period.

Up and down Britain I travelled to various Maranatha prayer groups for nine months calling on people to repent. The Lord had promised as people repented, the darkness over the whole of Ireland would be broken up. Little by little the darkness is breaking up. Though to date there is comparative peace in Northern Ireland, there is still a considerable way to go.

It was just after Christmas, when the Lord told me I was going to get married again. Now this was not what I wanted to hear. I felt I needed marriage, like I needed a hole in my head! However, after my protests had died down, I said OK Lord you know best, but I don't want to meet anyone until I have finished travelling around with the Northern Ireland message. The Lord told me I had six months to get the job finished and that is what I did.

I AM HEALED

In March I was asked again to go with the Maranatha team to Northern Ireland. On the final day of the visit the Lord healed me completely. That day we were in Portadown, a man came into the meeting, "I'm not staying" he said", He had just come to say he hated the British. We as a team had spent a great deal of our time in Ireland on our knees and faces as we repented on behalf of our nation, Britain. Now the tears flowed as we wept and asked for forgiveness from this man and those present. This town had known great tragedies, young people's lives sacrificed needlessly, this poor man was beside himself with grief and pain, but as we held him and asked for forgiveness, the Holy Spirit moved on him and set him free from the bitterness, grief and pain that had been his portion. He accepted our repentance and left the meeting rejoicing, healed and restored. I too felt the healing power of the Holy Spirit flow through me, and was healed and restored to life, set free from M.E..

Toward the end of my travels I became concerned that I had not been able to travel to the south of Ireland. As I prayed about it I felt the Lord saying leave that to me. There was no door open to visit that part of the land, so that was that. Some months later I received a letter from a Priest in Southern Ireland telling me he had received a copy of the call to repentance. This had been sent to him from someone in Northern Ireland. This little touch from the Lord to encourage me, letting me know repentance was coming to the South of Ireland too. Sometimes I wonder when Ireland will become one nation again, as when the Lord gave me this word I had a picture of the whole of Ireland covered with one flag. Since then I have met others who have also seen the whole of Ireland covered with one flag.

CHAPTER 17

Marriage was something I was definitely not considering. I was content to be on my own. I had rebuilt my life with the Lord's help. I was satisfied with the way things were going, the Lord was my husband and I was very happy with the arrangement.

However, the Lord had spoken quite clearly and simply when He said "you are going to get married again." It was not the most exciting news I had heard, but as I happen to believe that the Lord knows what is best for me, I am happy to trust Him in these matters. Even though like Moses I am prone to protest!

So I knew when the Lord said I was to be married, I knew from past experience that if He said it, it would be so. I also knew I could trust Him to work it out. The only thing I asked was that I would not meet my prospective husband until I had finished travelling. I still had six months of travelling around to do and I didn't feel I wanted the distraction of developing a new relationship at the time when I was travelling so much. I preferred to be single minded about what I was doing.

SCOTLAND

Easter week was spent in the highlands of Scotland, as part of a team praying around the clock for revival in Britain and sharing the word with believers in the area. We stayed in a beautiful spot outside a small seaside village. I had driven up with a friend and the team stayed in a lovely bungalow overlooking a river and the hills. Herds of deer roamed the area, and they would often cross in front of the car as we drove off the beaten track when we were off duty from praying.

The battle that week was very intense. The area we were staying in had been a sea port where the Scots had been deported from Scotland to Ireland during the time of the highland clearances. The pain and grief were still there as we stood at what had been the quay side; we could almost hear the cries of those being torn away from their homeland. Warring in the highlands was rife in those days. I met a young lady who had been married for about seven years. She told me that her husband had reminded her every day since they had married that his clan had beaten her clan four hundred years previously! You can understand when I say sadly that their marriage was breaking down. As we prayed for revival in Britain we were encouraged with signs in the heavenlies. One day there was a rainbow, right in front of the house, with both ends in the river. Then on another day the clouds parted to reveal a perfect map of Britain. The Lord's promise was that revival would come to the land.

LONDON

In June, Lance Lambert was speaking at Westminster Chapel in London. Ever since the group from our fellowship had been to Israel, I had wanted to encourage them to find out more about Israel, so that they could pray in a more informed way for the land and its people. There was to be five or six of us going to London. It was going to be a long day leaving our home town at six in the morning and returning after midnight. We were within a few days of going when several people began to drop out. It came to the point were there was only two of us left, a man named George and myself. Did he still want to go to the meeting I asked; he said he did. So I booked the tickets. Secretly however I was not looking forward to spending so much time with one man, to be honest I was terrified! I confided in a close friend, who agreed to pray for me, and my fears disappeared. We had a great day in London. Lance Lambert's teaching was excellent, and we were both challenged by what we heard. On the way home George asked me to go out with him at a later date. He had a dinner to attend in October and he could take a friend with him. That was almost four months away.

BACKGROUND

George and I had joined— or in my case rejoined, the same fellowship within a month of each other. He had newly come to know the Lord through a neighbour, who suggested he joined the fellowship. When finally some weeks later we were introduced to each other, he said he thought he knew me from some where. He did, we had lived across the road from each other, when we were children. He had been a friend of one of my brothers. Here we were nearly forty years later and he remembered me, but only because he says, I wasn't very nice to him, so he had been scared of me! Younger brothers can be a pain in the neck to teenage girls and mine was no different, as were his friends!

George and I often worked on the same teams in the church we were both involved in evangelism, which meant anything from prayer walking to taking the Jesus video out, to organising bistro meals. The meals were held on a monthly basis, Sunday evening event that members of the fellowship could invite their unsaved family and friends, to hear the gospel in an unthreatening environment. George was also part of the group from our fellowship that I took to Israel. We enjoyed working together and each other's company, beyond that, who was to know what the Lord was doing. I wasn't aware that George had been praying for a wife, 'Like Helen' he said to the Lord, readers please note he said 'like Helen,' not Helen. So when the Lord said "Why not Helen" this came as a bit of a shock to George. After all I had been a Christian for nearly thirty years and he for only two years. Because I taught Bible class, he thought I was too good for him! However I didn't know all this at the time. I realised that I was becoming attracted to him, so I stopped sitting next to him, lest I should grab his hand during a sermon! When we had gone to

London for the day, George asked me to let him know if there were any other Christian events elsewhere that I was attending as he was keen to learn more of the Lord. He had also asked me to help him buy plants for the garden he was developing, as he had no knowledge of plants and bushes. As I love gardening I agreed to visit the Garden centre with George and help him select the plants he needed. This is one of my favourite pastimes and spending someone else's money was even more rewarding.

GARDENING

Just after this the Lord told me to stay at home and worship Him on my own. I have to say after more than thirty years of attending church on Sunday, it seemed very strange indeed, but I checked it out with a Pastor I knew and he agreed that for a season that was what I was to do. So I informed my Pastor and elders of my intention to withdraw from the fellowship for a season, and we agreed to review the situation two months later.

Very soon I began to get telephone calls from George asking where was I? Why was I not at church? Would I still be doing his garden? So I explained the situation to him. Following a series of telephone calls we arranged to visit a local garden centre to buy the plants and bushes that were needed to fill George's garden. It is a big garden, so several visits later, the garden was beginning to look really well. The garden had been completely devoid of any flowers or plants except a backdrop of mature trees and bushes on all sides. It gave me the opportunity to experiment. In reading gardening books I had discovered that a long garden, similar to George's looked more square in shape by planting a hot border on one side and a cool border on the opposite side. That is what we did, we planted all the flowers that were warm colours together, like reds, yellows and oranges and all the cool colours like pink, blue lilac and white together. The whole effect was lovely having planted the plants out the garden was finished. During this time we had been growing closer together, George asked me to go out for a meal with him. We had a pleasant evening together, but I realised that I had a real problem. How could I ever trust a man again? Suddenly the past came back and hit me between the eyes. However, I had to trust the Lord who knew what was best for me. Later that month I had arranged to go with some friends to a conference held by the Pentecostal churches in the Northwest of England. The meetings where held in a university, over a four day period. My friends and I had been previously to these meetings and the teaching had been excellent. When I told George we were going, he asked if he could come too. What we didn't know was that we had both asked the Lord for the same thing which was if we were meant to be together long term, during this particular time away together, our relationship would take off and grow— and it did.

A THREE STRAND CHORD

The Lord said now you can go back to the fellowship. The first Sunday I was back, as we stood side by side worshipping. I saw a gold cord wind its way around us in the form of a figure eight. Then the words came A three strand cord is not easily broken, I knew the Lord was saying I'm doing this, and I am in this with you. The decision to get married came naturally to both of us, but we were both scared of the commitment. So much so, that when we decided to get married, we decided that neither of wanted to dress up. We would have the ceremony on a Sunday morning as part of the morning service. Our thinking was, that way we wouldn't need to wear anything special, But the Lord had other ideas. We arranged the date of the wedding for two months ahead.

However, before that there was another trip to Israel for me — my third that year.

CHAPTER 18

I was in Israel to prayer walk, like many intercessors I was called to walk the Land and cover it with prayer, coming before the throne of God for ten days or however many days the Lord required. My place for walking and praying was Jerusalem, and I would spend my days walking the streets seeking the Lord on behalf of the people. In Israel you can meet many intercessors, just there to serve the Lord in this way. Sometimes the Lord has His people walk specific areas. Other times it is to pray for specific events. Sometimes we are called to be there just for the Lord.

ARE YOU THERE?

Often we do not realise that the Lord has need of the fellowship of His children. Just weeks before I left for this visit to Israel, George and I were praying with a friend of ours, when we heard the Lord saying to each of us, "Who will be there for Me." It had not occurred to us that our Heavenly Father had needs. A need for his children to stop asking, and start giving to Him. Giving Him the worship and praise He so rightly deserves, like our earthly children who when they are young and all too frequently when they are not so young, come to us wanting something from us, not to give love and affection, but rather just to keep receiving. We are like that with our heavenly Father. He tells us He knows what we need, we don't need to keep asking. He is happy to grant us our requests as and when appropriate. However, to think of being there just to meet His needs is something He wants us to come into. As a parent, how would we feel if our children only ever came to us when they wanted something from us, rarely saying they loved us? We would feel sad and wonder at their lack of maturity. God wants us to grow into full maturity. To have the same relationship with Him that Jesus has with the Father. Jesus said 'I and the Father are one,' He meant one in spirit, one in heart and mind. He wants this for us so that we will come into the Sabbath rest, spoken of in the book of Hebrews chapter 4 v 4; for anyone who enters God's rest also rests from his own works, just as God did from his. V11, Let us, therefore, make every effort to enter his rest, so that no one will fall by following their example of disobedience.

ENTER MY REST

Looking back into the book of Hebrews chapter three, we find that from v 7 up to v 7 of chapter four the Lord says three times; Do not harden your heart when you hear My voice, if you do You will not come into the promised land. Who was the Lord talking to? The children of Israel whom Moses was leading into the promised land. It is frightening to think of it, but why did only two men of those who left Egypt, Joshua and Caleb, get into the promised land, when more than two million people left Egypt forty years before? Sadly, because they hardened their hearts toward the Lord they did not enter His rest. Three times in these verses we see that the Lord is saying, they shall never enter my rest. Why? Because of their rebellion. They kept hardening their hearts toward the Lord. They were not obedient, and there comes a time when the Lord says to all of us, enough. If you won't cease from doing your own thing, your own works, then He will say to us, you shall never enter My rest. He wants us to rest from our labours, and do nothing at all that He has not planned and purposed. Often we fail to hear Him say, who will be there for me, which is a pity because we lose some of the greatest blessings we can ever know on this earth.

SIT AT HIS FEET

To sit at the feet of the Lord, on Mount Zion, is to have a foretaste of heaven, Sitting at Jesus' feet is something we can all do, if only we will, step off the everlasting wheel of service. Service, He often hasn't ordained. To be like Mary, whom Jesus said had the better part by sitting at His feet. This is what we are called to do, this is our ultimate destination, to sit at His feet. There is no point in thinking we will start practising later if we don't learn to do it now, when we get to heaven it will be too late. Is He saying to you; Martha, Martha, you are worried and upset about many things, but only one thing is needful. To sit at His feet to enjoy His presence. For Him to enjoy your presence and for you to know His peace. His joy and the wonderful warmth of His love.

CHAPTER 19

In Israel as I waited upon the Lord, He began to speak to me about the wedding. To my surprise He told me what kind of wedding clothes we were to wear, these were not as we had planned!

I was to wear a long white dress, embroidered with lace, gold and pearls. George was to wear a proper wedding outfit. These clothes were to be symbolic, of how we need to have the right clothes to come into the Kingdom of God. In the book of Revelation chapter nineteen v 8; Fine linen, bright and clean was given her to wear (Fine linen stands for the righteous acts of the saints). Who was to wear this robe, the bride of Christ. We were to dress symbolically, to remind us that one day as the bride of Christ we will wear such garments. When we know Jesus Christ as our Lord and Saviour, we are given a robe of righteousness, by our bridegroom, Jesus.

WHITE ROBES

In Israel, in Jesus' time, the bridegroom presented his bride with a plain white robe. The bride was expected to embroider the robe before the bridegroom came for her. She had to be diligent about this task if she was to have a beautiful robe. She did not know at what time the bridegroom would return for his bride. When we receive our robe of righteousness we are to embroider our robe with the righteous acts ordained for us, since before time began. These, as we have seen, are mentioned in the first book of Corinthians chapter three. Paul talks about, gold, silver and precious stones, which are indicative of the works the Lord has planned and purposed we should do. When we do our own thing, we cease to embroider our robes. If we come into His rest we will be making our robes beautiful for when our heavenly bridegroom comes to claim His bride.

For more years than I care to remember, I had had no desire to wear a white wedding dress, but when the Lord spoke, it was different. Gone was whatever had given me an unpleasant feeling at the thought of wearing such a dress. When this happened to me I understood how God had created the heavens and the earth. He just said it and it was so. When I told George what the Lord said about the wedding clothes we had to wear, as he said. "Yes Lord," he was healed too.

A RING

The Lord went on to tell me what flowers I was to carry and the colour. Perhaps the most amazing thing was when he spoke about the wedding ring I was to wear. The Lord told me it was to be of three shades of gold, this was to remind us that this marriage was not just about the two of us, but that He was part of it too. The ring was to serve as a reminder in the difficult times that He had bound us together Back home from Israel, George and I had six weeks to organise the wedding. The very next day we set off to a neighbouring town to look for rings and other items needed for the wedding. It wasn't a town we were very familiar with. So we parked the car in the shopping precinct car park and walked down to the shopping mall. We had looked for the type of ring the Lord had described in our home town but we couldn't see anything remotely resembling the ring the Lord had described to me. We came out of the stairwell of the car park and walked across to a jewellers shop opposite the exit. There in the first shop we went to was the ring just as the Lord described. We went in the shop and I tried the ring on having made arrangements to have it adjusted we paid for it and had left the shop within fifteen minutes." While we are here, I said to George, "let's go to a dress fabric shop, I know". The shop sold, paper dress patterns and fabrics. We went into the shop, and there were a pile of pattern books, I picked one up, opened it at the appropriate section and there on the first page was the dress the Lord had spoken to me about. That was how all the arrangements for the wedding went. Three weeks before the wedding, David my eldest son told me that Kate, his eldest child, who was six at the time, wanted to know if she could be a bridesmaid.

BRIDESMAIDS

We had planned to have just an adult bridesmaid and best man in attendance. Small children had not been in the scheme of things. In addition, we had eleven grandchildren at the time, ten of them under six years of age. We couldn't have one without the others. Several of the children were babies or toddlers at the time, some didn't want to take part. So we ended up with two small girls and two small boys as attendants. What would they wear? The boys were easy enough we could hire outfits to match the best man and George's outfits. However, we thought the girls would be problem. We went to a wedding outfit shop I knew, walked into the shop and there hanging on the rack were two small dresses, in white, with exactly the same coloured sashes as the Chief bridesmaid was to wear. When they tried them on, they fitted perfectly. The Lord proved yet again that, when he tells us to do something, he knows where everything is if only we will listen. So we were ready, fully clothed just as the Lord had planned, feeling very happy and comfortable with all that the Lord had done.

The ceremony was on Remembrance Day and it was certainly a day to remember. Surrounded by family, fellowship and friends, we were married.

CHAPTER 20

After our marriage we moved into George's bungalow. While the bungalow was not the house I saw in the vision. There were many elements of it that I had seen in the vision that Gary Stephenson had told me previously; that the vision could prove to be elements of several houses and so it was.

George's bungalow was detached, the drive was on the left. The house had a beautiful large back garden. But amazingly, it was the bathroom just as I had seen in the vision; green bath, toilet, and wash basin. The walls were tiled and the wood was pine , including the ceiling, just as I had seen, all those years before. You might think that because I had seen this bathroom many times previously, that I would make a connection between this house and the vision. I can say in all honesty that despite the fact I had visited George's house many times prior to our engagement, I had never been aware of the colour scheme of that room until after we had agreed to marry. But where were all those other bathrooms and bedrooms I had seen?

THE CALL

We received many scriptures on our marriage from friends and well wishers. One in particular spoke to us it came from the book of Ezekiel chapter 3 v 4; Go now to the house of Israel and speak my words to them. The Lord had given us these same words just a few weeks previously, when we, as part of our fellowship, had been away for a teaching weekend. George and I had both made notes and both had recorded this same scripture. From the day of our marriage we sought the Lord regarding this call.

DEPRESSION

George returned to work after our honeymoon. Within days he had to stay home from his work, for depression had set in. He had had this problem in the past. It was a family problem and his father before him had suffered from the same illness. With it came the tears. Tears flowed for months sometimes he wept for most of the day other times just for a few hours, but for months; there wasn't a day went past when he didn't weep. The Lord was healing him from the grief and pain of the past. With the help of our Pastor and his wife we were able to minister healing and deliverance to George as the Lord revealed the many damaged areas of his life.

I hadn't worked for more than five years now through my own fight with M.E. and the weakness it has left me with. Now George and I were together twenty four hours a day. This went on for eight months. The Lord was restoring the years the locust had taken away making George into a new man. Our Pastor's wife once commented that the Lord changed both of us in such a short time, that we were like different people.

ISRAEL AGAIN

A few months later the Lord began to speak to us about visiting Israel, there He said He would speak to us. We booked our flights and packed our bags, this time together.

WITNESSING

We had been in Israel for a week before the Lord spoke to us. We had decided to go on a tour of the Knessett, the Israeli Parliament building. While on our tour the young Israeli girl, was sharing with us some of the detail of the Chagall tapestries , that adorned the wall of the Knessett. The Holy Spirit began to speak to me, as our guide explained that Chagall's wife was a believer. This had influenced him in the design of one of the tapestries, which was based on the New Testament scriptures. She confessed that she didn't know what several of the scenes depicted. As the Holy Spirit led me, I was able to take her on one side and explain several of the scenes she could not understand. Particularly the portrayals of Yeshua—Jesus as the lion of Judah, which is very prominent in one of the tapestries. We ended by sharing the gospel with her, as depicted in the Chagall tapestries.

AGAIN

The next day was our last full day in Israel. We needed to go to Ein Karem, the home town of John the Baptist. My younger son wanted us to collect some items for him from the Biblical Resource centre in that village. We were on the bus going to Ein Karem when a young American man started to speak to us. He asked us why we were in the land. We explained to him that we were Christian believers in Jesus. He told us that as a Jew he could not understand why Jesus had to come; he thought God had done all that was required. As the Holy Spirit led me, I was able to take him through the blood sacrifice system that God had given to Moses for the Children of Israel. The blood sacrifices were implemented so that the sins of the people could be atoned for. When Jesus died on the cross, his blood was shed once for all for our sins. Jesus' blood cleanses us from all sin as it had every generation since his death when people looked to him for forgiveness. In the book of (Isaiah chapter fifty—three) it talks of the suffering servant and the price he paid. I recommended this chapter to the young man. Though many Jews are discouraged from reading this particular chapter of Isaiah. However, I recommended that he read the chapter where he would be able to recognise Yeshua—Jesus from what was written there. We left him as he went on to discover the Chagall windows at the Hadassah hospital.

AND AGAIN

We continued on our journey, our mission completed in the

village, catching the bus going on to Yad Vashem, the Holocaust Museum. Two ladies sat in front of us on the bus, turned and said "I recognise that accent", and started to talk to us. We got off the bus at Yad Vashem together. One of the ladies told us she had converted to Judaism. Once more the conversation turned to Jesus and again I was sharing the gospel with the ladies, going through the sacrificial system yet again. As we parted company from the ladies, George and I reflected on how wonderful it had been to share the gospel with three different Jews. Truly the Lord was reinforcing to us that we were called to teach the Jews and thankfully we were to teach them in our own language.

Back home in England we both felt we should return to work. George felt well enough to work a regular day shift, but not the twenty four hour shift system he had worked for the past twenty six years. The Lord opened the way for me to work with small businesses again and I was able to work from my office at home most of the time; visiting companies as and when I was required. For me this was a good way of working. I still had days when I was very tired, but as I worked from home, I was able to set my hours to the state of my health.

JEWISH ROOTS

George and I were increasingly being challenged as Christians, about our Jewish roots. After all we knew the first Christians were Jews. The New Testament was based on the Old Testament that was God's word to the Jews. Everything about our faith is rooted in Judaism as God laid it down and has been recorded in the Old Testament. The Torah, as the Jews call the first five books of the Old Testament, in addition to the writings and the prophets. When we look at the New Testament, we see many of the scriptures quoted are directly from the Old Testament. Jesus and Paul frequently quoted the Old Testament. They were both Jews, as trained rabbis they knew the word of the Lord.

When Jesus appeared to the two men on the road to Emmaus after His resurrection, we are told in Luke chapter 24 vs 25-27; How foolish you are, and how slow of heart to believe all that the prophets have spoken. Did not the Christ have to suffer these things and then enter his glory? And beginning with Moses and all the prophets, he explained to them what was said in all the scripture concerning himself. Jesus in his resurrection body, had appeared to them and proceeded to read the scriptures to them, which scriptures? The Old Testament. We as Christians have been deceived into disassociating ourselves from the Jews and Israel. To our cost we have abandoned our Jewish roots —for what? A form of Christianity without roots. If we disassociate ourselves from our roots then how can we say our roots are in Jesus? His roots are in Judaism, for He was, and is, a Jew. We can't turn Jesus into the blue-eyed, blond-haired man we have so often seen in the paintings from the past. Jesus was a Jew from Israel and was quite probably dark eyed, dark skinned, with dark hair. While scripture does not tell us what He looked like, we only have to look at native Israelis to catch a glimpse of what He could have looked like.

CHAPTER 21

George and I had the opportunity of taking part in a course to learn more about our Jewish roots. The course was residential and lasted a week. Run by Christian Friends of Israel in Britain, the "Kesher Course" as it is known, was very helpful and we were able to use what we had learned to help others seeking the truth concerning their roots. Immediately we came back from attending the course, the Lord spoke to us. Independently, we were told to sell the house. So we put the house up for sale.

ISRAEL BECKONS

Within weeks I noticed an advertisement in the Christian Friends of Israel news sheet, the advertisement stated that they needed a cook for their Jerusalem office. I jokingly said to George if I had been single I would have applied for the position. His reply came as a surprise. "Why don't you apply, I can always leave the Post Office and work in the CFI distribution centre?" We faxed my details to the Jerusalem office, who responded by asking for more details, also whether George would be willing to work as a maintenance man doing the repairs etc on the premises. 'Yes' George would be willing.

George was working for the Royal Mail. He had worked for them for twenty-six years. He decided to ask for a career break. This was granted to him initially for two years, which was later extended to three years. He wouldn't be paid but would have a job to return to when we returned to Britain.

Two months went by and we heard no more from the application we had made to Christian Friends of Israel. We felt increasingly that the Lord was calling us to Israel. We had to make a decision as the Royal Mail made it quite clear that by the beginning of January they wanted to know what George was going to do. We prayed and sought the Lord again. We knew we had enough money to live in Israel for six months without needing to work. We felt we should step out in faith and go. George gave notice at work that he would be absent from the end of January, and we stepped out. Within days we received a fax from Christian Friends of Israel inviting us to join their staff as a cook and maintenance man. Soon we were on the way. The house hadn't been sold, so we rented it to a couple who eventually bought the house.

WORKING

Having previously made six visits to Israel within the last three years, it was like a second home to me, except that this time we were there to work. Cooking lunch for twenty-five people became a joy for me. It was hard work, but just as the Lord had said his yoke was easy and His burden light. Jesus was true to His word, for His yoke is easy and His burden is light for He is the burden bearer if we are yoked to Him. Just as with the oxen when they pull together, the work is easy, for it is a shared burden. When the Lord had prepared us for a work, He has equipped us for that which He has called us to.

Christian Friends of Israel is one of many support organisations that are in Israel to help the Jews and the Arabs. CFI as they are known is there mainly to help the Jews. Christians in many parts of the world send shipments of clothing and household items to help those Jews making aliya (returning to their homeland of Israel). Often they can only bring with them the usual amount of luggage allowed by the airlines. When you are emigrating, a suitcase of possessions is not sufficient. Organisations like CFI help by providing the extra essentials needed to set up home. When Jews return to their homeland the Israeli government gives them a small amount of money each week that only covers their basic needs. Clothing is a major problem for many families. It is a great blessing for them to be able to go to a distribution centre for a supply of clothing, bedding or household items.

APPRECIATION

Despite the fact that the Lord had equipped us to do the work, we were incredibly tired for the first three months. We simply worked and slept; there was no energy for anything else. Gradually we acclimatised, and discovered a life outside of work. One of the great blessings of those days, were the staff we cooked for, particularly the Americans; they were so appreciative of all that George and I did. For George and me this was quite overwhelming at first. Neither of us had been used to being blessed and encouraged in that way. One day it took me all my time not to burst into tears, when a lady told me how much she appreciated my cooking. I had been cooking since the age of ten. For I was the eldest of a large family. Never before had what I did been so appreciated. George too grew in stature as he was praised for his efforts in the organisation. He was being asked to do many repair jobs that he had never undertaken before. We would always pray about the tasks allotted to us and the Lord by His Spirit would enable us to complete everything satisfactorily.

THIS IS ISRAEL

Israel is a very tiring country, fast moving and very noisy. To live there is quite a trying experience. During our early days in the land the words most frequently on our lips, was,' this is Israel'. Whether it was the furniture in the first apartment we had, whether it was our first landlord's response to anything and everything. Always the thought would be 'this is Israel'; this country has a culture all its own. In some aspects of life, it is twenty years or more behind Western society. In other aspects it is so advanced it amazes you. Certainly, to live there is an experience, never to be forgotten.

JOURNEYS

We travelled to work each day by bus. Buses have two speeds in Israel, fast and stop there is nothing in between. Consequently, if you completed your journey without injury you were blessed indeed. Each morning George and I lurched our way to work in this stop, go, fashion, frequently getting off the bus before we arrived at our destination, either because of the constant traffic jams, or because one of us thought we would be sick if we stayed on any longer. Queues are non existent in Israel. If you are waiting for a bus, you may be first in line, but you will be last on the bus if you don't adopt the ploys of the experts who are usually advanced in years. The elderly are experts at getting on the bus first. The trick is to use your elbows, the bonier the better. Believe me when you have spent many years practising this art form it really does work for you. Children learn very quickly. You can stand at a bus stop especially in the areas of schools and there will not be a child in sight. Then the bus appears and at the same time so do hoards of children, who immediately push their way to the front of the queue and climb on the bus. They will push you out of the way and sadly most of the children that do this come from religious Jewish families. In the shops it is just the same, you may have managed to get the attention of one of the shop assistants, when several other shoppers will interrupt while you are being served. You are immediately forgotten while they deal with those who have pushed in. No order, just he who shouts loudest, or pushes the hardest gets the attention. Being English was no help at all. We are far too polite as a nation to succeed in this culture, but we are learning!

CULTURE SHOCK

Driving a vehicle is another culture shock! Recently I read this comment by an American Jew regarding the driving skills of Israelis in general. Herman Wouk in his book, 'This is my God' had this to say about his fellow Jews, "The Israeli driver on the open road is not a driver at all, but an aeroplane pilot who cannot quite get off the ground owing to the lack of wings, yet he never stops trying." He goes on to encourage us to believe that in these modern times the speed of the traffic has diminished. My response to that would be where? In the cities it is an education driving a car, especially in Jerusalem. This is where George was in his element. We would use the company van to visit the market, known as the shouk, for the company's supplies. There's nothing George enjoys more, than a fight with a car, and its driver. Israeli driving is right up George's street— anything they can, do he can do better. So many of the cars in Jerusalem have dents in their body work. Nobody seems to bother getting them repaired so consequently the attitude seems to be, if I get another bump, so what!

LOOK NO HANDS

To drive in Jerusalem, you need nerves of steel, and quick reactions, not to manoeuvre the car quickly out of the way of other vehicles, but to hit the horn! Most drivers use one hand for the horn and the other for gesticulating, while he's leaning out of the window telling you what he thinks of you. Fortunately, our Hebrew is not up to translating what he is saying, however his hands say it all. "Look no hands" takes on a totally new meaning when driving in Israel. In four lane traffic, it is not unusual to move from the fourth lane to the first, in one move! This may be carried out anywhere, from standing at the traffic lights to driving down the motorway. Prayer is the key to life in Israel along with a sense of humour.

Within weeks of arriving in Israel the Lord started to speak to us about getting a larger house in the city. "Enlarge your tent," then He repeated it again, "Enlarge your tent," how? where? Oh Lord, here we go again.

CHAPTER 22

We had been in Israel just six weeks, when the Lord told us to find a bigger place and move into the city. We set about looking at various agents lists of properties, newspapers etc, trying to find a larger place. As with every thing else, finding an apartment or house in Israel is not straight forward. We all get used to the system in our own country, discovering how it is done. In another land it is another ball game. Different agents require different commissions, terms of agreements, as anywhere else in the world.

THAT'S IT LORD

We looked around, but saw nothing we liked. Then we met an agent who was easier to talk to than many, and through him we almost rented a larger property in the city centre, but right at the last minute on the day we were due to sign the lease, the owners started moving the goal posts, making demands that we were not prepared to agree to. "That's it Lord," we said, "if you want us to move you will have to find us a place." "Ha" said the Lord," just what I have been waiting for you to say!"

Several weeks later, some friends of ours came over from England and in the course of having a day out with them they introduced us to a couple who were from Australia, but were now returning to their homeland. They had an apartment they needed to find tenants for. We went around to look at it, and fell in love with it immediately. This is it, no hassle with agents, no fees to pay, just what we needed.

However, there were several things to do with the tenancy agreement that we were not happy with. We asked the Lord to give us favour with the landlady so that those elements of the agreement we felt we could not agree to, would be accepted by the landlady. The Lord moved on her and we had the terms we required.

LITTLE HOUSE

We loved our little house, which was like a double detached garage, one storey, similar to our bungalow in England. The house sat at the end of a driveway, with apartment blocks on each side. Every window of the house overlooked someone else's garden, wonderful for us, a garden; but no gardening, just what we needed. However, the Lord had said a larger house this one was smaller, but we felt it was what the Lord wanted for us at this time. The situation of the property was ideal. For those who know Jerusalem it was in the street next to the YMCA. It was an easy walk to work; in fact we never needed to travel on a bus again, thank you Lord!

Still the Lord was speaking to us about getting a bigger house. All we could say was, 'Lord if you want us to move into a bigger house you will have to do it, just as you brought us here, so Lord find this bigger place for us.' We sat back and waited enjoying our little house and the lovely gardens that surrounded us. The grape vine outside the lounge window was a constant source of pleasure to us, as were various birds who ate their way through the grapes. That was until the owners of the vine decided to put brown paper bags on each bunch of grapes and then we had the joy of watching the birds trying to peck their way through the bags— often succeeding!

A BIGGER HOUSE

We had arranged to go back to England in July for a short break. We still had not sold our house in England and the lease was due to expire shortly. Also the Lord had been speaking to us concerning disposing of the remnants of our possessions. Before we left England to live in Israel we had given most of our furniture away. We had but a few small household items and books in boxes these we had left in the basement of the manse belonging to our fellowship. Now the Lord was telling us to dispose of the remainder of our possesions.

Our landlady came to collect the rent before we left for our holiday in England. She casually asked if we knew anyone who wanted to rent a large house in the Old City, in the Jewish quarter in Jerusalem. I equally casually asked if we could use it as a bed and breakfast. "Oh yes" was her eager response. We discovered that the house had been Olga and Ilan's family home, they had brought their six children up there. The previous year they had decided to move out of their home in the Old city, to the outskirts of new Jerusalem city on the edge of the countryside. They had let the house to tenants for a year. They were disappointed with the lack of care and respect that had been shown for the property, so much so that Ilan could no longer bear to visit the house, even to collect the rent. Now they had given the present tenants notice to quit and were looking for new tenants. We said that we might be interested in moving into the house, but as we were leaving for England within the next two days we did not feel that we could spare the time to visit the property. If the house was still available when we returned in a month's time, we would visit the property with a view to renting it. Meanwhile, we prayed, if this house is what you want for us, then let it still be available when we return.

CONFIRMATION

While we were in England our fellowship held a prayer meeting for us. During the meeting one lady, who is an intercessor, told us she had had a picture of a house in a very strategic position. Never having been to Jerusalem she had no idea how the Old city was divided up. However, with her hands she showed us that she had seen a house at a strategic junction. We thanked her for this revelation we had no idea at the time just how accurate her description of the house was to be.

When we returned to Israel, we contacted Olga, our landlady, who informed us the house in the Old city was still available. We made arrangements to view it a few days later. We arrived to find absolute mayhem. It is impossible to describe the state of the house. We could hardly put a foot on the floor for debris, toys, plates of food, dirty nappies and just about every mortal thing you could think of. In addition, doors were hanging off their hinges, walls were covered with drawings crayoned by the children. The present tenant had done nothing to tidy the place up for our visit, we could only imagine that this had been done as a deterrent to put us off taking the place. Whatever the motive was it didn't work! We could see beyond the mess and damage to the potential beauty of the place. We knew without a shadow of doubt that this was the house the Lord wanted for us.

STRATEGIC POSITION

The house is one of the few remaining not damaged during the 1948 and 1967 wars, which had destroyed much of the Jewish quarter of the Old city of Jerusalem. The house is just inside the Jewish quarter. The Arab or Muslim quarter, as it is known is at the junction at the bottom of the street. The picture our friend from our fellowship had seen was correct, this was a strategic junction. The house is more than five hundred years old and originally it had been two Arab houses. The first occupant had been employed to keep the graveyard on the Mount of Olives clean and tidy when it was built.

The battle to take possession of the house had yet to begin. The enemy of our souls was not going to let us into the house that easily. Three months were to pass before the present tenants were to move out. They were not happy that their tenancy agreement was not going to be extended to a further year . Olga and Ilan were not happy with the extent of the damage that had been done. For a while it was stale mate, all we could do was pray, which we did along with those who were standing with us in prayer. Then we received a telephone call from Olga to say that the tenants had moved out. We could now start cleaning the place up and repairing the damage, along with our small army of helpers.

How to publicise the bed and breakfast was a problem as we really didn't know many people. We contacted some of the organisations in Jerusalem who were helping the people of the land. We had just one hundred leaflets printed and sent them to everyone we knew in England. We also sent several to Christian organisations and we still had some left!

Our first visitor was a Jewish lady from Argentina. As Christians heard of our venture they recommended us to their friends. Soon people came from every continent, just through one person telling another.

CHAPTER 23

Many Christians are offended at the thought of being rewarded by the Lord for service to Him. Reward is not a dirty word. If we love our children and they have been helpful to us, we will often give them some sweets or a gift as a reward, so our Heavenly Father likes to reward His children, when they do something for Him.

THE REWARD

1 Corinthians chapter 3 v 14 says; if what he has built survives the fire, he will receive his reward. Here it explains that in the last day the day of judgement the works we have carried out in the name of the Lord will be judged by fire. What is not of the Lord will be burnt up, but what is of the Lord will remain, and there will be rewards for those surviving works. Why baulk at the thought that we will receive rewards when we get to heaven? Jesus says much about carrying out the tasks allotted to us and the rewards to be gained by those who are faithful. In Luke chapter 12 v 42, Jesus is recorded as saying; Who then is the faithful and wise manager, whom the master puts in charge of his servants to give them their food allowance at the proper time? It will be good for that servant whom the master finds doing so when he returns. I tell you the truth he will put him in charge of all his possessions.

When those made responsible for handling money, as recorded in Luke chapter 19 vs 12-17, were congratulated for making money, they were given responsibility for cities, many cities.

When we look at the rewards mentioned in the Bible, we begin to see that in heaven too, we will have responsibilities. Many people do not think about what they will be doing in heaven. Others think they will be worshipping the Lord all day long. While I am sure we will be worshipping continually. There will also be work delegated to us in the new heaven and on the new earth. We are now being prepared for those heavenly responsibilities .

BE FAITHFUL

The disciples will be judging the twelve tribes of Israel, and eating and drinking. Jesus speaks of this in Luke chapter 22 v 28; You are those who have stood by me in my trials. And I confer on you a kingdom, just as my Father conferred one on me, so that you may eat and drink at my table in my kingdom and sit on thrones, judging the twelve tribes of Israel.

The book of Revelation has much to say concerning our future, our eternal future. In chapter 2 v 7 we are told; if we conquer, we will eat from the tree of life in paradise; V10 states if we are faithful unto death we will be rewarded with a crown of life. In v 17; If we overcome we will receive some of the hidden manna, and a new name. Power over nations will be given to him who overcomes and does the Lord's will.

Perhaps you are like me, have little strength and feel that you can't hold on. Read chapter three of the book of Revelation there is encouragement there for you in v11. I am coming soon. Hold on to what you have, so that no one will take your crown. V 12 Him who overcomes I will make a pillar in the temple of my God. Never again will you leave it. I will write on him the name of my God and the name of the city of my God, the new Jerusalem, which is coming down out of heaven from my God; and I will also write on him my new name. These wonderful promises are for you if you will be obedient and follow in the way the Lord has ordained for you. Finally, if we overcome, we will sit on the throne with Jesus, seated at the right hand of God and reign with Jesus in the heavenlies for eternity. However, those rewards are only for those who are found faithful to the end and overcome all obstacles by His grace and mercy. How do we overcome? Revelation chapter nine v 6 tells us it is by the word of the Lord, by our testimony and the blood of the lamb.

Finally the book of Romans tells us, God will give to each person, according to what he has done.

The eternal destiny of all those who love the Lord, is to be in His presence for eternity. It is no good thinking that you will look forward to that day, when you don't practise now. If you are not prepared to be like Mary and sit at His feet now, you will not be ready to sit at His feet eternally.

CHAPTER 24

The waiting indeed was over! Here we were looking out over this amazing scenery that had hardly changed in thousands of years. It was like a dream. After waiting for more than sixteen years here in front of me was the outcome of the vision the Lord had given all those years ago.

THE LORD DOES IT

The house has five bedrooms, just as the Lord had shown me it would have. There is a bedroom on the first floor and several bathrooms and wash rooms. Strangers do come to our door, just as He had promised. Within weeks of opening the bed and breakfast people had visited the house from every continent. Mostly they came by word of mouth, being recommended by someone from another country. We are amazed at the power of God to communicate through His people. We have a ministry house just as the Lord foretold. People come from all over the world to minister to the people of this land. Jews and Gentiles alike stay in the house. They in their turn minister to Jews and Arabs as they are called to do by the Lord. We minister to them, by taking care of their bodily needs and also by praying for healing and protection for them, when we are asked to do so.

WE ARE AMAZED

As we gaze from our roof top garden, we are truly amazed at what the Lord has done to bring us to this point in time and to this place. For this is His house on His mountain, for this house is sitting on Mount Zion the Lord's Holy Mountain the place of His habitation. Here as we look out over the Mount of Olives, the Western Wall known as the Wailing wall, and Mount Moriah, where the Dome of the Rock is situated. We stand in awe of Him who promised, planned and purposed we would serve Him on His Holy mountain.

However, His plans and purposes are not just about buildings and ministries. This is a road I have been walking along for more than thirty five years A walk that required me to take up my cross daily, to die to self and live for Him — our precious Lord Jesus Christ. His plans and purposes are for each one of us and that includes you dear reader, God the Father has a plan to conform us to the image of His son, Jesus is the first born of many brethren. We are called to be made in His image if only we will allow Him to do the work in us that is needed to transform each one of us.

IT COST HIM

When Jesus laid down His life it cost Him, He paid the price for our sins. It cost Him to be separated from His Father, as He took our sin upon Himself. It cost Him to become the Son of man, to lay aside all the power He had as the Son of God. However, it was a price He was willing to pay for us. We were called to be like Him. Though not to take on the sins of the world but to be conformed to His image.

How to be like Him in character is described, in the 2 Peter chapter 1 vs 3-11; His divine calling has given us everything we need for life and godliness through our knowledge of Him who called us by His own glory and goodness. Through these He has given us His great promises, so that through them you may participate in the divine nature and escape the corruption in the world caused by evil desires. For this reason, make every effort to add to your faith goodness, and to goodness, knowledge and to knowledge, self control and to self control perseverance and to perseverance godliness, and to godliness, brotherly kindness and to brotherly kindness, love. For if you possess these qualities in increasing measure, they will keep you from being ineffective and unproductive in your knowledge of our Lord Jesus Christ. But if any one does not have them, he is nearsighted and blind, and has forgotten that he has been cleansed from his past sins. Therefore, my brothers, be all the more eager to make your calling and election sure. For if you do these things, you will never fall, and you will receive a rich welcome into the eternal kingdom of our Lord and Saviour Jesus Christ.

Our Heavenly Father is anxious that we take on His Holiness, the same Holiness which Jesus has. We are to develop the same character as Jesus, because we are called to be sons of God. Walking as Jesus walked, having the same relationship with the Father as Jesus had with him. We are to be Holy as He is Holy. We are called to bear fruit, fruit that abides. What is fruit we may ask? Again, we are called to be like Jesus, bearing much fruit. Paul's letter to the Galatians chapter 5 vs 22-26, tells us more about the fruit the Lord desires to see in our lives; But the fruit of the spirit is love, joy, peace, patience, kindness, goodness, faithfulness, gentleness and self control. Against such things there is no law.

GRAPES AND WINE

When we look at the grape and then look at a bottle of wine, we realise that there has been some process that has taken a bunch of grapes and turned them into wine. The main process is one of squeezing the grapes to extract as much juice from them as possible, so it is in our lives, the only way to extract the fruit of the Spirit from us is by squeezing us. Eventually we will be squeezed so hard it will hurt, really hurt. If we are to die to self it means sacrifice, sacrifice costs you. Denying yourself means not being there for your children, when they need you. Sacrifice can mean giving up everything you have to follow Jesus. However, when we look at what Jesus gave up to bring us into the Father's eternal presence can we refuse, His call to follow Him?

When I view the exterior of the house in Jerusalem it looks nothing like the house I saw in the vision, as Gary Stevenson had predicted. If I had seen a house like this in the narrow streets of the Jewish quarter, within the confines of the Old City of Jerusalem when I originally let the vision go, I probably would not have taken it up again. The reason I say this is that I was very much a home bird and to see the exterior of this building, in this city at that point of time in my life would have filled me with such fear. One of the changes the Lord has wrought in me over the years, is a willingness to die to my self. I have always enjoyed home life, just as I was content to be married to one man for life. For my life to turn out as it has, with so much rejection from men has been a mystery to me. However, despite it all, my love of the Lord has grown stronger and stronger.

Writing this book has given me the opportunity to look back on my life and ask the Lord why so many of these trials came my way. There is no ready answer, except I had to walk this path so that I could write this book— to share His blessings with others who like me are just ordinary people who have an extraordinary God. The Lord had said some thirty years ago that I had to live the life he had for me before I could write about it.

NO LUCK, CHANCE AND FATE

What happens in God's scheme of things if He has a plan and someone is unwilling to fit into this plan? A few days ago while reading the United Christian Broadcasting's study notes I came across this reading; "There are three words you need to drop from your vocabulary right away; luck, chance and fate. Instead use the word 'providence' It means to see in advance and provide for". It continued, You can't improve on the Westminster Confession, written in the 17th century. Listen "God the creator, doth uphold, direct, dispose, and govern all creatures, actions and things from the greatest event to the least, by His most wise and Holy providence."

Aren't you glad that He is still in charge?

You may say," what about our human will? Can't we act independently?" R.C. Sproul writes, "God's sovereign providence stands over and above our actions. He works out His will through the actions of human wills, without ever violating the freedom of those wills"

YOU MEANT EVIL

Look at Joseph, his brothers tried to destroy him, but their efforts only put him on the throne, and fulfilled the will of God. Later, Joseph said, you meant evil against me, but God meant it for good in order to bring about this present result. (Gen. 50 v 20 NAS) It was Judas's worst act of wickedness that helped bring about the best thing that has ever happened, the atonement. Are you confused by the things going on around you? That's because we only use ten per cent of our mental potential, because we know only in part (1 Cor 13 v9). Someday, God will explain it all to us. Until then, trust Him and rejoice, because " He's got the whole world in His hands" and that includes you.!

This book has been about how the Lord turned my life upside down, because I dared to love Him and follow Him whatever the cost. My heart's desire has always been to serve the Lord, but increasingly I have discovered the best way to serve Him is to do His will, to do only what He desires me to do, which is to sit at His feet.

With all that is within you, desire to arrive at a place where you can sit at His feet. If this was a place that we all could cope with He would compel us to do just that, but He won't force us to do something. However, He will work in our lives so that we desire to do just that. Dear reader if I could encourage you in just one thing, it would be to fulfil His will and sit at His feet. This is our ultimate destination.

CPSIA information can be obtained
at www.ICGtesting.com
Printed in the USA
BVHW092203200521
607797BV00005B/853